Virginia
Bed
&
Breakfast
Cookbook

Happy Cooking!
Melissa Craven

Virginia Bed & Breakfast Cookbook

Second Edition

ISBN 1-889593-14-1

Printed in China

Design: Lisa Bachar
Editing: Susan Larson

Cover Photos:
The Inn at Warner Hall, Gloucester, Virginia (top)
©Thomas Firak Photography / StockFood (bottom)

3D Press, Inc.
2969 Baseline Road
Boulder, CO 80303
303-623-4484 (phone)
303-623-4494 (fax)
info@3dpress.net (email)

888-456-3607 (order toll-free)
www.3dpress.net

Introduction

The Bed & Breakfast Association of Virginia invites you to experience Virginia hospitality at its finest. We invite you to enjoy a delicious selection of the favorite or most requested recipes of our member Bed & Breakfast Inns. Our recipes are like our inns – some are "down home," while others feature more sophisticated flavors. Every recipe is well worth your time and tasting, so sit back and enjoy!

The Virginia Bed & Breakfast Cookbook will introduce you to the wide variety of beautiful inns in Virginia. All offer the time-honored tradition of gracious Southern hospitality. We invite you to enjoy our special combination of wonderful food, great conversations and excellent accommodations. Nothing gets you closer to the romance, history and natural beauty of Virginia than the ambiance of a Virginia B&B. We offer romantic getaways, historic homes and rustic retreats in cities and small towns alike.

Visit Our Mountains … The Shenandoah Valley offers the beautiful Shenandoah National Park's Skyline Drive and further south the famed Blue Ridge Parkway. Miles of scenic beauty, with waterfall overlooks and beautiful vistas make the western edge of Virginia a lovely destination.

Watch History Come Alive … Explore historic Jamestown, Yorktown and Williamsburg, and visit the largest living history museum in the country. Visit central Virginia and tour the homes of Presidents Jefferson, Madison, Monroe and Wilson. Travel to northern Virginia and see the nation's capitol, the home of George Washington and the Smithsonian museum.

Enjoy Beautiful Water Ways … Travel old country roads along the many rivers and streams that flow though Virginia. Visit the Eastern Shore, the ocean and even small islands where the villagers step back in time. Fish, sail and dine on fresh oysters, clams and our famous crab cakes.

Visit a winery, a Civil War Site or a Historic Plantation … Stay awhile and enjoy the beauty and the hospitality of Virginia. You can see and do it all while visiting a Virginia Bed & Breakfast Inn. See all that we have to offer by visiting us on the internet at www.innvirginia.com.

Thank you for giving us the opportunity to share our hospitality with you!

Eleanor Ames
President
The Bed & Breakfast Association of Virginia

Acknowledgements

Creating a book is a work involving many people. We owe a great deal of gratitude to the following friends, family members and business colleagues for their support, inspiration, enthusiasm, time and talents:

Susan Larson, Eleanor Ames, President of the Bed & Breakfast Association of Virginia, Danelle Previd, Pete Schroeder, our official taste-testers and a special thank you to the owners, innkeepers and chefs of the 94 Virginia bed & breakfasts and country inns who generously and enthusiastically shared their favorite recipes and beautiful artwork.

Table of Contents

Breads, Muffins & Biscuits

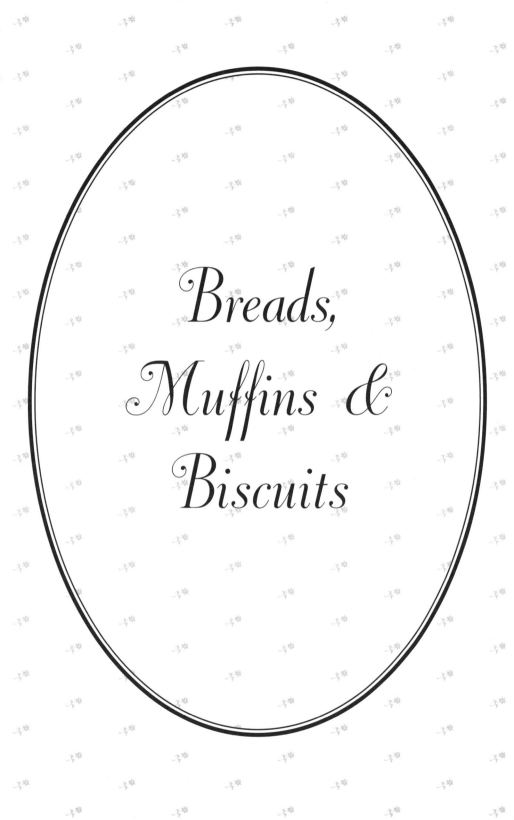

Breads, Muffins & Biscuits

Old Courthouse Inn

The Old Courthouse Inn is a historic farmhouse located 30 minutes from Charlottesville and an hour from Richmond. Monticello and Ash Lawn are only 20 minutes away – see them both and still be back in time for afternoon tea! For historians, Appomattox is just over an hour away. There are also several excellent wineries within easy driving distance.

Set on 35 private acres, with woods, a fishing pond and open pastures, the original house was built in 1777 and served as a tavern. Remains of the county's original courthouse and jail can still be seen on the property.

INNKEEPERS:	Gene & Cindy Ann Trentacosta
ADDRESS:	12330 James Madison Highway
	Palmyra, Virginia 22963
TELEPHONE:	(434) 589-1977
E-MAIL:	cindyann@oldcourthouseinn.com
WEBSITE:	www.oldcourthouseinn.com
ROOMS:	3 Rooms; 1 Suite; Private baths
CHILDREN:	Children age 12 and older welcome
ANIMALS:	Not allowed; Resident dog & cats
HANDICAPPED:	Not handicapped accessible
DIETARY NEEDS:	Will accommodate guests' special dietary needs

Strawberry Bread

Makes 6 Small Loaves

"This is a great recipe because you can get the most out of strawberries when they are in season and cheap – just hull and freeze them until needed. When I mix up a batch, I freeze some of the batter and thaw and bake it as needed." ~ Innkeeper, Old Courthouse Inn

3   cups all-purpose flour
2   cups sugar
1   tablespoon cinnamon
1   teaspoon baking soda
½   teaspoon salt
3   large eggs
1   cup canola oil
3   cups sliced fresh or frozen (thawed and drained) strawberries

Preheat oven to 350°F. Lightly grease 6 mini-loaf pans. In a large bowl, combine flour, sugar, cinnamon, baking soda and salt. In a medium bowl, beat eggs well until foamy. Beat in oil. Stir in strawberries. Fold egg mixture into flour mixture until flour mixture is moistened.

Divide batter among pans (batter can be frozen at this point, defrosted and baked later). Bake for 35 minutes, or until a toothpick inserted in center comes out clean. Remove loaves from oven and cool on wire racks for 5 minutes. Remove loaves from pans, slice and serve warm.

Belle Hearth

B elle Hearth Bed & Breakfast is located in the historic district of Waynesboro, a small town in the Shenandoah Valley, just two miles from the Blue Ridge Parkway and Skyline Drive entrances. With its gabled roof, wrap-around porch with swing, heart-pine floors, pocket doors and seven fireplaces, the Belle Hearth depicts the fine craftsmanship of the late Victorian/Neo-Classical period.

At breakfast, you will find the dining table set with silver and old china – the perfect backdrop for the inn's old-fashioned country fare.

INNKEEPERS:	Linda & Wayne Mielczasz
ADDRESS:	320 South Wayne Avenue
	Waynesboro, Virginia 22980
TELEPHONE:	(540) 943-1910; (866) 710-2256
E-MAIL:	bellehearth@yahoo.com
WEBSITE:	www.bellehearth.com
ROOMS:	3 Rooms; 1 Suite; Private baths
CHILDREN:	Children age 8 and older welcome
ANIMALS:	Not allowed
HANDICAPPED:	Not handicapped accessible
DIETARY NEEDS:	Will accommodate guests' special dietary needs

Hawaiian Banana Nut Bread

Makes 2 Loaves

"Guests love this moist, flavorful bread. It can be served at breakfast or as an accompaniment to afternoon tea." - Innkeeper, Belle Hearth Bed & Breakfast

3	cups all-purpose flour
½	teaspoon salt
1	teaspoon baking soda
2	cups sugar
1	cup chopped pecans or walnuts
3	eggs, beaten
1	cup vegetable oil
2	cups mashed ripe banana
2	teaspoons vanilla extract
1	(8-ounce) can crushed pineapple, drained

Preheat oven to 350°F. In a large bowl, combine flour, salt, baking soda and sugar. Stir in nuts. In a medium bowl, combine eggs, oil, banana, vanilla and pineapple. Add egg mixture to flour mixture and stir just until flour mixture is moistened.

Divide batter between 2 greased and floured 9x5-inch loaf pans. Bake for 70 minutes, or until a toothpick inserted in center comes out clean. Cool bread in pans for 10 minutes, the remove from pans and cool completely on a wire rack.

Shepherd's Joy

S ituated in the historic district of Abingdon (the oldest incorporated town west of the Blue Ridge), Shepherd's Joy offers an opportunity to experience the rare Victorian charm of an in-town working sheep farm. The Queen Anne country-style home was built in 1892 and has been lovingly restored, melding the old with the modern conveniences of today.

Escape to Shepherd's Joy to rest, relax and enjoy the pleasures of an unhurried life. Join your fellow guests on the wrap-around porch or stroll the grounds and admire the peacefulness of sheep grazing in the pasture.

INNKEEPERS:	Jack & Joyce Ferratt
ADDRESS:	254 White's Mill Road
	Abingdon, Virginia 24210
TELEPHONE:	(276) 628-3273
E-MAIL:	stay@shepherdsjoy.com
WEBSITE:	www.shepherdsjoy.com
ROOMS:	4 Rooms; Private baths
CHILDREN:	Children age 10 and older welcome
ANIMALS:	Not allowed
HANDICAPPED:	Not handicapped accessible
DIETARY NEEDS:	Will accommodate guests' special dietary needs

Carrot Zucchini Bread

Makes 2 Loaves

"This bread is delicious for tea spread with whipped cream cheese and topped with a light sprinkling of freshly grated ginger." ~ Innkeeper, Shepherd's Joy

3	large eggs, beaten
1	cup vegetable oil
2	cups sugar
1	cup grated zucchini
1	cup grated carrot
2	teaspoons vanilla extract
3	cups all-purpose flour
1	teaspoon baking soda
½	teaspoon baking powder
1	teaspoon salt
1	teaspoon cinnamon
½	cup chopped pecans
½	cup shredded coconut

Preheat oven to 325°F. Line 2 (9x5-inch) loaf pans with waxed paper (or grease and flour). In a large bowl, beat eggs. Mix in oil, sugar, zucchini, carrots and vanilla. In a medium bowl, whisk together flour, baking soda, baking powder, salt and cinnamon. Add flour mixture to egg mixture and stir until combined. Fold in nuts and coconut.

Divide batter between pans. Bake for 1 hour, or until a toothpick inserted in center comes out clean. Cool bread in pans for 10 minutes, then remove from pans and cool completely on a wire rack.

Caldonia Farm - 1812

C aldonia Farm - 1812 is a magnificent Federal-style home located on a working cattle farm adjacent to Shenandoah National Park. The house was built of native fieldstone in 1812 and is on the National Register of Historic Places. A full candle-lit breakfast of eggs Benedict, smoked salmon, custom omelets and more is served at an hour of your choice.

With advance notice, innkeeper Phil Irwin will arrange for limo service, hot air balloon or aircraft rides, fishing, battlefield or historic guides, horse and carriage rides, theater tickets and other special activities.

INNKEEPERS:	Phil Irwin
ADDRESS:	47 Dearing Road
	Flint Hill, Virginia 22627
TELEPHONE:	(540) 675-3693; (800) 262-1812
E-MAIL:	Not available
WEBSITE:	www.bnb1812.com
ROOMS:	2 Suites; Private baths
CHILDREN:	Children age 12 and older welcome
ANIMALS:	Horses allowed
HANDICAPPED:	Not handicapped accessible
DIETARY NEEDS:	Will accommodate guests' special dietary needs

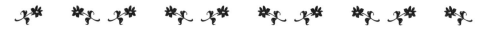

Apple Nut Bread

Makes 1 Loaf or 12 Muffins

2	cups all-purpose flour
¾	cup sugar
1	tablespoon baking powder
1½	teaspoons baking soda
1½	teaspoons cinnamon
1	large egg
2	tablespoons vegetable oil
1	cup applesauce
1	cup chopped nuts

Preheat oven to 350°F. Grease a 9x5-inch loaf pan. Combine flour, sugar, baking powder, baking soda and cinnamon. Add egg, oil and applesauce; mix well. Stir in nuts. Pour batter into pan. Bake for 45 minutes, or until a toothpick inserted in center comes out clean. Cool on a wire rack.

Oak Grove Plantation

The air revives you as you approach Oak Grove Plantation, down its sienna-colored lane lined with loblolly pines. The air is alive with the sounds of the country. Guests enjoy sipping tea on the front porch on a lazy summer day. The same family that greeted visitors to this antebellum home in the 1820s welcomes you with Southern hospitality 180 years later.

A gourmet breakfast is served each morning in the Victorian dining room. Entrées may include Cluster Spring egg puff or lemon soufflé pancakes, served with locally grown fruits and homemade biscuits or muffins.

INNKEEPERS:	Pickett Craddock
ADDRESS:	1245 Cluster Springs Road
	Cluster Springs, Virginia 24535
TELEPHONE:	(434) 575-7137; (877) 343-7871
E-MAIL:	info@oakgroveplantation.com
WEBSITE:	www.oakgroveplantation.com
ROOMS:	3 Rooms; 1 Suite; Private & shared baths
CHILDREN:	Welcome
ANIMALS:	Dogs welcome; Resident dog
HANDICAPPED:	Handicapped accessible
DIETARY NEEDS:	Will accommodate guests' special dietary needs

Sally Lynn

Serves 24

"This is my mother's recipe for a Southern favorite." ~ Innkeeper, Oak Grove Plantation Bed & Breakfast

½	cup milk
¾	stick butter
½	teaspoon salt
2	large eggs
1	package (2¼ teaspoons) active dry yeast
¼	cup warm water (105-115°F)
2	tablespoons sugar
2	cups white or whole-wheat pastry flour

In a saucepan, heat milk just to the boiling point, then remove from heat. Add butter and salt; stir until butter is melted and combined, then cool to lukewarm. Put eggs in a food processor; pulse to beat well. In a small bowl, combine yeast, warm water and sugar; stir to dissolve yeast and let stand until foamy. Add yeast mixture, lukewarm milk mixture and flour to food processor; pulse to mix well, then cover and let rise until doubled in size.

Preheat oven to 400°F. Spray a Bundt pan with non-stick cooking spray. Pour batter into pan, cover and let rise until doubled in size. Bake for 20 minutes, or until a toothpick inserted in center comes out clean. Cool in pan for 10 minutes, then remove from pan and cool completely.

The Inn at Sugar Hollow Farm

The Inn at Sugar Hollow Farm is a country bed & breakfast on 70 acres, surrounded by picturesque mountains, majestic hardwood forests and rushing streams. Located west of Charlottesville, the inn is adjacent to the Blue Ridge Mountains and Shenandoah National Park, and a short drive from Monticello and the University of Virginia.

Whether you choose to explore nearby areas, go on historic or winery tours, shop or take a soothing walk beside a woodland stream to absorb the peace of the natural habitat, your stay will be both relaxing and memorable.

INNKEEPERS:	Dick & Hayden Cabell
ADDRESS:	PO Box 5705
	Charlottesville, Virginia 22905
TELEPHONE:	(434) 823-7086
E-MAIL:	innkeeper@sugarhollow.com
WEBSITE:	www.sugarhollow.com
ROOMS:	7 Rooms; Private baths
CHILDREN:	Children age 12 and older welcome
ANIMALS:	Not allowed
HANDICAPPED:	Not handicapped accessible
DIETARY NEEDS:	Will accommodate guests' special dietary needs

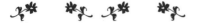

Cranberry Crunch Muffins

Makes 12 Muffins

"These are great to serve during the holiday season as the cranberries yield bright dots of red in the muffins. Our guests, however, enjoy them throughout the year. Fresh cranberries freeze well and can be stirred into the batter while frozen. This recipe can easily be doubled for more guests." ~ Innkeeper, The Inn at Sugar Hollow Farm

3	cups all-purpose flour
¾	cup sugar
1	tablespoon baking powder
½	cup milk
1	stick butter or margarine, melted
2	large eggs
1	tablespoon vanilla extract
1½	cups fresh or frozen cranberries
¾	cup chopped pecans or walnuts
1	tablespoon grated orange zest (optional)

Preheat oven to 375°F. Combine flour, sugar and baking powder. Make a well in center of flour mixture. Add milk, butter, eggs and vanilla to well and stir gently just until moistened. Add cranberries, walnuts and orange zest (if using frozen cranberries, add them last as they will chill the dough and make it hard to stir). Fill greased or paper-lined muffin cups ⅔-full. Bake for 25-30 minutes, or until muffins spring back when gently pressed.

The Foxfield Inn

B ed chambers at the Foxfield Inn are uniquely designed to provide a memorable experience. All rooms are on one floor and offer complete privacy. The creamy yellow Garden Room features a two-person Jacuzzi, remote control fireplace, cherry four-poster canopy bed and bay window. Guests enjoy woodland and mountain views. An outside porch is just steps away for relaxing after your busy day in Charlottesville.

"In all my more than 50 years of traveling, I've never stayed in nicer accommodations." ~ Guest, Australia

INNKEEPERS:	Mary Pat & John Hulbert
ADDRESS:	2280 Garth Road
	Charlottesville, Virginia 22901
TELEPHONE:	(434) 923-8892; (866) 369-3536
E-MAIL:	info@foxfield-inn.com
WEBSITE:	www.foxfield-inn.com
ROOMS:	5 Rooms; Private baths
CHILDREN:	Children age 14 and older welcome
ANIMALS:	Not allowed
HANDICAPPED:	Handicapped accessible
DIETARY NEEDS:	Will accommodate guests' special dietary needs

Lemon Raspberry Streusel Muffins

Makes 12 Muffins

2	cups all-purpose flour
½	cup sugar
½	teaspoon baking soda
2	teaspoons baking powder
½	teaspoon salt
1	(8-ounce) carton raspberry yogurt
½	cup vegetable oil
1	teaspoon grated lemon zest
2	large eggs
1	cup fresh or frozen (unthawed) raspberries

Streusel topping:
⅓	cup sugar
¼	cup all-purpose flour
2	tablespoons butter

Preheat oven to 400°F. In a large bowl, combine flour, sugar, baking soda, baking powder and salt; mix well. In a small bowl, combine yogurt, oil, lemon zest and eggs; mix well. Add yogurt mixture to flour mixture and stir just until dry ingredients are moistened. Gently stir in raspberries. Fill greased muffin cups ¾-full.

Sprinkle streusel topping over batter. Bake for 18-20 minutes, or until light golden brown and a toothpick inserted in center comes out clean. Cool muffins for 5 minutes, then remove from pan. Serve warm.

For the streusel topping: Combine sugar and flour. Using a pastry blender or a fork, cut in butter until mixture is crumbly.

Note: If using frozen raspberries, you may need to break them up if they are frozen together.

Ivy Creek Farm

I vy Creek Farm Bed & Breakfast, an eight acre country estate, is just five minutes from colleges, shopping, restaurants, hospitals and country clubs, and 15 minutes from historic downtown Lynchburg. Indulge in Ivy Creek Farm's warm hospitality, gracious service and bucolic setting, along with the farm's memorable gourmet breakfasts and luxurious accommodations.

Relax on the expansive veranda overlooking the woods and pond. Watch deer and birds. Or venture into the local environs of the foothills of the Blue Ridge Mountains where history, activities and natural beauty abound.

INNKEEPERS:	Marilyn & Lynn Brooks
ADDRESS:	2812 Link Road
	Lynchburg, Virginia 24503
TELEPHONE:	(434) 384-3802; (800) 689-7404
E-MAIL:	info@ivycreekfarm.com
WEBSITE:	www.ivycreekfarm.com
ROOMS:	2 Rooms; 1 Suite; Private baths
CHILDREN:	Children age 12 and older welcome
ANIMALS:	Not allowed; Resident dog
HANDICAPPED:	Not handicapped accessible
DIETARY NEEDS:	Will accommodate guests' special dietary needs

Pumpkin Chocolate Chip Muffins

Makes 12 Muffins

"My daughter was given this recipe and she passed it on. These are good make-ahead muffins as they taste better the next day." - Innkeeper, Ivy Creek Farm

½	cup sliced almonds
1⅔	cups all-purpose flour
1	cup sugar
1	teaspoon baking soda
½	teaspoon baking powder
1½	teaspoons cinnamon*
¼	teaspoon nutmeg*
¼	teaspoon ground cloves*
¾	teaspoon mace*
¼	teaspoon salt
2	large eggs
1	cup canned pumpkin
1	stick butter, melted
1	cup chocolate chips

Preheat oven to 350°F. Put almonds on a baking sheet or in a pie pan and bake for about 5 minutes, just until lightly browned. Grease muffin cups or line with muffin papers.

In a large bowl, thoroughly mix flour, sugar, baking soda, baking powder, cinnamon, nutmeg, cloves, mace and salt. In a medium bowl, combine eggs, pumpkin and butter; whisk until well blended. Stir in chocolate chips and almonds. Add pumpkin mixture to flour mixture and stir just until mixture is moistened (do not overmix).

Divide batter among muffin cups and bake for 20-25 minutes, or until a toothpick inserted in center comes out clean (muffins should still seem a little underdone when removed from oven).

*Note: You can substitute 2¾ teaspoons of pumpkin pie spice for the cinnamon, nutmeg, cloves and mace.

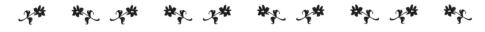

Brierley Hill

Situated on eight acres of grassy meadows overlooking the Shenandoah Valley, Brierley Hill welcomes guests to fine cuisine, gracious accommodations and spectacular views at reasonable prices. Located just five minutes from historic Lexington, the inn offers a quiet country respite for the weary traveler and a romantic getaway from the workaday world.

Brierley Hill was recently voted one of the top 25 inns in the United States in the book *America's Favorite Inns, B&B's & Small Hotels*.

INNKEEPERS:	Ken & Joyce Hawkins
ADDRESS:	985 Borden Road
	Lexington, Virginia 24450
TELEPHONE:	(540) 464-8421; (800) 422-4925
E-MAIL:	relax@brierleyhill.com
WEBSITE:	www.brierleyhill.com
ROOMS:	3 Rooms; 2 Suites; Private baths
CHILDREN:	Children age 12 and older welcome
ANIMALS:	Not allowed; Resident dog
HANDICAPPED:	Not handicapped accessible
DIETARY NEEDS:	Will accommodate guests' special dietary needs

Pumpkin Pecan Muffins

Makes 18 Muffins

1¼	cups old-fashioned or quick-cooking rolled oats
1	cup all-purpose flour
⅓	cup chopped pecans
1	teaspoon baking powder
1	teaspoon cinnamon
½	teaspoon baking soda
½	teaspoon salt
½	teaspoon nutmeg
1	cup canned pumpkin
¾	cup packed brown sugar
½	cup vegetable oil
¼	cup milk
1	large egg
1	teaspoon vanilla extract

Topping:

¼	cup old-fashioned or quick-cooking rolled oats
¼	cup all-purpose flour
¼	cup packed brown sugar
3	tablespoons chopped pecans
1	teaspoon cinnamon
½	stick butter, softened

Preheat oven to 400°F. In a large bowl, combine oats, flour, pecans, baking powder, cinnamon, baking soda, salt and nutmeg. In a medium bowl, combine pumpkin, brown sugar, oil, milk, egg and vanilla. Add pumpkin mixture to oat mixture and mix well. Fill greased or paper-lined muffin cups ¾-full. Sprinkle topping over batter. Bake for 15-20 minutes, or until done. Remove muffins from muffin cups and serve warm.

For the topping: In a bowl, combine topping ingredients.

Holladay House

T he circa 1830, Federal-style Holladay House in downtown Orange, is within walking distance of historical sites, restaurants, antique shops and art galleries. Only 90 minutes from Washington, D.C. and Richmond, Orange lies in the heart of fox hunting and steeplechase racing country.

Nearby Civil War battlefields, Montpelier, Charlottesville, Monticello, the University of Virginia, wineries, vineyards, fishing, the Blue Ridge Mountains, horse farms, the Skyline Drive and hiking and biking trails make deciding what to do the major topic over breakfast.

INNKEEPERS:	Judy Geary
ADDRESS:	155 West Main Street
	Orange, Virginia 22960
TELEPHONE:	(540) 672-4893; (800) 358-4422
E-MAIL:	jgearyhh@aol.com
WEBSITE:	www.holladayhousebandb.com
ROOMS:	4 Rooms; 2 Suites; Private baths
CHILDREN:	Children age 12 and older welcome
ANIMALS:	Welcome; Resident cats
HANDICAPPED:	Not handicapped accessible
DIETARY NEEDS:	Will accommodate guests' special dietary needs

Pete's Buttermilk Biscuits

Makes 10 to 12 Biscuits

"I have tried many biscuit recipes, but these are the best!" ~ *Innkeeper, Holladay House Bed & Breakfast*

2	cups all-purpose flour
1	tablespoon baking powder
2	teaspoons sugar
½	teaspoon cream of tartar
¼	teaspoon baking soda
¼	teaspoon salt
1	stick butter, chilled plus ½ stick butter, melted
¾	cup buttermilk

Preheat oven to 450°F. Sift together flour, baking powder, sugar, cream of tartar, baking soda and salt into a bowl. Cut in the 1 stick of chilled butter until mixture resembles coarse crumbs. Make a well in center of flour mixture; add buttermilk all at once and stir just until dough clings together.

Gently knead dough about 10-12 times on a floured surface. Pat dough out to ½-inch thick. Cut dough with a 2½-inch biscuit cutter or a glass. Dredge biscuits in the ½ stick of melted butter. Bake for 10-12 minutes, until golden.

Linden House Plantation

The Linden House Plantation Bed & Breakfast is a restored 1750s planters-style home. It is listed on the National Register of Historic Places and is a state landmark. The lush grounds boast walking trails, an English garden and a gazebo, as well as a stocked fishing pond. Guests are encouraged to relax on any of the six porches or sitting areas located on the grounds and enjoy a tall glass of freshly made lemonade.

A full plantation breakfast includes country biscuits, ham biscuits, muffins and breads and one of Sandy's great omelets or Ken's famous Belgian waffles.

INNKEEPERS:	Ken & Sandy Pounsberry
ADDRESS:	11770 Tidewater Trail
	Champlain, Virginia 22438
TELEPHONE:	(804) 443-1170; (866) 887-0286
E-MAIL:	lindenh@crosslink.net
WEBSITE:	www.lindenplantation.com
ROOMS:	5 Rooms; 2 Suites; Private baths
CHILDREN:	Children age 12 and older welcome
ANIMALS:	Not allowed; Resident cat & dog
HANDICAPPED:	Not handicapped accessible
DIETARY NEEDS:	Will accommodate guests' special dietary needs

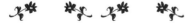

Easy Beignets

Makes 16 to 24

"We were hosting a Mardi Gras party and were pressed for time to come up with a menu of New Orleans foods. At the grocery, we saw tubes of biscuits and thought we'd experiment — they worked like a charm!" ~ Innkeeper, Linden House Plantation Bed & Breakfast

Oil, for frying
1   (8-ounce) tube flaky biscuits
Powdered sugar

Heat oil in a deep fryer or a deep skillet to 350°F. Separate biscuits and pull or tear each biscuit in half. Fry biscuits for about 30 seconds per side; drain on paper towels. Put powdered sugar in a plastic bag. Add beignets, a few at a time, and shake in bag to dust with powdered sugar. Serve.

Strathmore House on the Shenandoah

Come and enjoy the Strathmore House Bed & Breakfast, a beautifully restored 1892 Victorian gem. Occupying possibly the Shenandoah Valley's most spectacular location, overlooking the historic Meems Bottom Covered Bridge and the North Fork of the Shenandoah River, this local landmark invites guests to step back in time and experience life as it might have been in a more romantic and gracious era.

Once the hub of an extensive apple orchard enterprise, guests now come for excellent accommodation and matchless breakfast cuisine.

INNKEEPERS:	Kay & Jim Payne
ADDRESS:	658 Wissler Road
	Mt. Jackson, Virginia 22842
TELEPHONE:	(540) 477-4141; (888) 921-6139
E-MAIL:	strath@shentel.net
WEBSITE:	www.strathmorehouse.com
ROOMS:	4 Rooms; Private baths
CHILDREN:	Not allowed
ANIMALS:	Not allowed; Resident cat
HANDICAPPED:	Not handicapped accessible
DIETARY NEEDS:	Will accommodate guests' special dietary needs

Quick Butter Croissants

Makes 32 Croissants

"My guests love these. They can be frozen after baking, thawed and reheated in a 250° oven." ~ Innkeeper, Strathmore House on the Shenandoah

1 cup warm water plus 1 tablespoon water
1 package (2¼ teaspoons) active dry yeast (not "rapid rise" yeast)
5 cups all-purpose flour, divided
¾ cup evaporated milk
2 eggs, divided
⅓ cup sugar
1½ teaspoons salt
½ stick butter, melted plus 2 sticks butter, chilled

Put the 1 cup of warm water in a medium bowl. Sprinkle yeast over warm water and let stand for 5-10 minutes to soften. Beat 1 egg and add to yeast mixture along with 1 cup of flour, evaporated milk, sugar, salt and ½ stick of melted butter; stir until smooth. Put remaining 4 cups of flour and 2 sticks of chilled butter in a large bowl. With a pastry blender or two forks, cut butter into flour until butter is size of kidney beans. Add yeast mixture and stir just until flour is moistened. Cover tightly with plastic wrap and refrigerate for at least 4 hours or for up to 4 days.

Form dough into a ball and put it on a lightly floured board. Knead dough about 6 times (there will still be sizable pieces of butter in dough). Divide dough into 4 parts and roll each part into a 17-inch circle. Cut each circle into 8 wedges. Roll up each wedge into a crescent shape starting at the wide end. Put croissants on an ungreased baking sheet. Cover with a tea towel and let stand at room temperature for 1 hour, or until doubled in size. Preheat oven to 325°F. Mix remaining 1 egg with the 1 tablespoon of water; brush over tops of croissant. Bake for about 35 minutes, until golden (be careful not to overbake, croissants burn easily). Serve warm.

Coffee Cakes, Scones & Granola

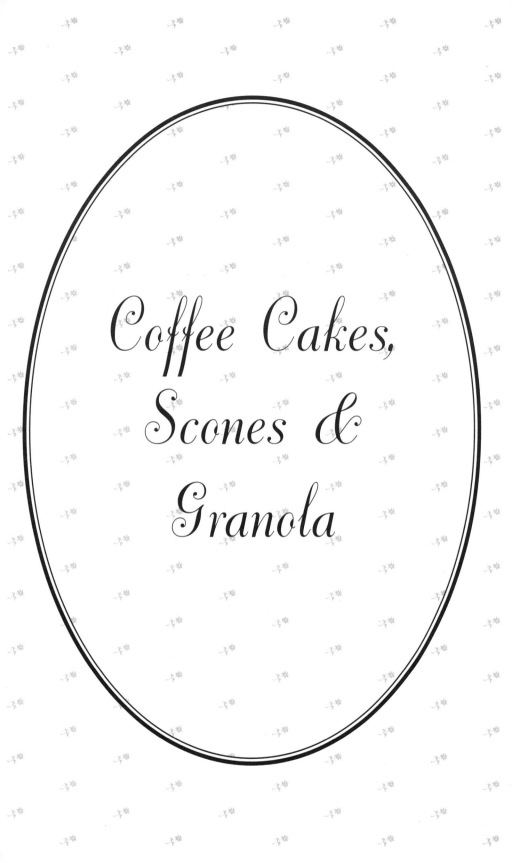

Coffee Cakes, Scones & Granola

The Inn at Narrow Passage

The oldest guest rooms at the Inn at Narrow Passage feature pine floors, stenciling and a Colonial atmosphere. Newer rooms are decorated in the same style, but open on to porches, with views of the Shenandoah River and the Massanutten Mountains.

After a busy day of hiking or sightseeing, return for lemonade on the porch in summer or hot spiced tea by the fire in winter. In the morning, the inn's hearty breakfast will get your day off to a great start.

INNKEEPERS: Ellen & Ed Markel
ADDRESS: Route 11 South at Chapman Landing Road
                  Woodstock, Virginia 22664
TELEPHONE: (540) 459-8000; (800) 459-8002
E-MAIL: innkeeper@innatnarrowpassage.com
WEBSITE: www.innatnarrowpassage.com
ROOMS: 12 Rooms; Private baths
CHILDREN: Welcome
ANIMALS: Not allowed
HANDICAPPED: Handicapped accessible
DIETARY NEEDS: Will accommodate guests' special dietary needs

Shenandoah Apple Cake

Makes 1 Tube Cake

"The Shenandoah Valley is well known for its apple orchards. This moist coffee cake also makes a lovely dessert." ~ Innkeeper, The Inn at Narrow Passage

5 Granny Smith apples, peeled and thinly sliced
2 tablespoons cinnamon
5 tablespoons plus 2 cups sugar
4 large eggs
1 cup vegetable oil
3 cups all-purpose flour
1 tablespoon baking powder
2½ teaspoons vanilla extract
Juice of 1 orange (about ¼ cup)

Preheat oven to 350°F. Grease and flour a large tube cake pan. In a medium bowl, combine apples, cinnamon and 5 tablespoons of sugar; toss to coat apples. In a large bowl, beat eggs and remaining 2 cups of sugar. Add oil, flour, baking powder, vanilla and orange juice; mix well. Alternate layers of batter and apples in pan, beginning with batter and ending with a decoratively arranged layer of apples. Bake for 70 minutes, until top is a deep golden brown and looks dry.

Bluemont

B luemont Bed & Breakfast's full country breakfast will help you start the day out right. Breakfast features an assortment of juices or special morning beverages, seasonal fruit dishes, muffins or pastry fresh from the oven and entrées such as four-cheese scrambled eggs *en croissant*, caramel pecan-stuffed French toast and Virginia smoked meats.

"This is by far the warmest, most hospitable B&B I have ever visited." ~ Guest, Bluemont Bed & Breakfast

INNKEEPERS:	Eleanor & Alfred Ames
ADDRESS:	1852 U.S. Highway Business 340
	Luray, Virginia 22835
TELEPHONE:	(540) 743-1268; (888) 465-8729
E-MAIL:	innkeeper@bluemontbb.com
WEBSITE:	www.bluemontbb.com
ROOMS:	3 Rooms; Private baths
CHILDREN:	Children age 12 and older welcome
ANIMALS:	Not allowed, Resident cats
HANDICAPPED:	Not handicapped accessible
DIETARY NEEDS:	Will accommodate guests' special dietary needs

Cinnamon Crunch Coffee Cake

Makes 12 Servings

"Every guest who tries this raves about it and asks for the recipe. The recipe can easily be halved and baked in an 8x8-inch pan. Plan ahead, the batter needs to be refrigerated overnight." ~ Innkeeper, Bluemont Bed & Breakfast

2	cups all-purpose flour
1¼	teaspoon baking powder
1	teaspoon baking soda
2	teaspoons cinnamon, divided
½	teaspoon salt
1	stick plus 2⅔ tablespoons butter
1	cup white sugar
1	cup packed brown sugar, divided
2	large eggs
1	cup buttermilk or sour milk*
1	cup chopped peeled Granny Smith apples
½	teaspoon nutmeg
½-¾	cup chopped pecans or walnuts

In a medium bowl, combine flour, baking powder, baking soda, 1 teaspoon of cinnamon and salt. In a large bowl, cream butter, white sugar and ½ cup of brown sugar. Add eggs and beat until fluffy. Add buttermilk and flour mixture alternately to butter mixture, mixing well after each addition. Fold in apples. Pour batter into a greased 9x13-inch baking pan. In a small bowl, combine remaining ½ cup of brown sugar, nutmeg, remaining 1 teaspoon of cinnamon and nuts; sprinkle over batter. Cover and refrigerate overnight.

The next morning, set pan on a countertop while preheating oven to 350°F. Bake cake for 35-40 minutes, or until a toothpick inserted in center comes out clean.

*Note: To make sour milk, mix 1 cup milk with 1 tablespoon lemon juice or vinegar and let stand for 5 minutes.

The Richard Johnston Inn

The 1700s were a time rich in history, independence and glorious homes. Come to the Richard Johnston Inn in Old Towne Fredericksburg to experience a unique, upscale 18th century inn. The inn was constructed by John Taylow, an architect and a signer of The Declaration of Independence. The Richard Johnston Inn still reflects the charm and grace of a past era, while providing all the amenities of today.

"A delightful bed & breakfast in the heart of the historic district." ~ *The Philadelphia Inquirer*

INNKEEPERS:	Bonnie L. DeLelys
ADDRESS:	711 Caroline Street
	Fredericksburg, Virginia 22401
TELEPHONE:	(540) 899-7606; (877) 557-0770
E-MAIL:	rjohnstoninn@staffnet.com
WEBSITE:	www.bbonline.com/va/richardjohnston
ROOMS:	9 Rooms; 2 Suites; Private baths
CHILDREN:	Welcome in 2 rooms
ANIMALS:	Welcome in 2 rooms; Resident dog
HANDICAPPED:	Not handicapped accessible
DIETARY NEEDS:	Will accommodate guests' special dietary needs

Sour Cream Coffee Cake

Makes 18 Servings

"Guests request this recipe often. It is very easy to make." ~ Innkeeper, The Richard Johnston Inn

1	stick butter, softened
1	cup sugar
2	large eggs
1	teaspoon vanilla extract
2	cups all-purpose flour
1	teaspoon baking powder
1	teaspoon baking soda
1	cup sour cream
1	(20-ounce) can pie filling, flavor of choice

Preheat oven to 350°F. Grease a Bundt pan well (an oblong bundt pan works well for ease of slicing). Cream butter and sugar. Add remaining ingredients, except pie filling, and mix thoroughly. Pour ½ of batter into pan. Spoon ¾ of pie filling over batter. Top with remaining batter, then remaining pie filling. Bake for 1 hour, or until a toothpick inserted in center comes out clean.

Smithfield Farm

S et in the hills of the Shenandoah Valley, Smithfield Farm commands a majestic view of fields and orchards, mountains and forests. The house is a classic 19th century manor, constructed of brick and stone with the traditional Federal period architectural style. Inside, an elegant, sweeping staircase adds beauty to the grand hallway, while spacious rooms are flooded with sunlight, reflected off the warm, hardwood floors.

"The house and farm are lovely and elegant, yet cozy. It was such a treat to be pampered with wonderful breakfasts." ~ Guest, Smithfield Farm

INNKEEPERS:	Ruth & Betsy Pritchard
ADDRESS:	568 Smithfield Lane
	Berryville, Virginia 22611
TELEPHONE:	(877) 955-4389
E-MAIL:	info@smithfieldfarm.com
WEBSITE:	www.smithfieldfarm.com
ROOMS:	3 Rooms; Private baths
CHILDREN:	Children age 12 and older welcome
ANIMALS:	Not allowed; Resident dog
HANDICAPPED:	Not handicapped accessible
DIETARY NEEDS:	Will accommodate guests' special dietary needs

Cinnamon Rolls

Makes 24 Servings

"Piping hot cinnamon rolls are our guests' favorite! They love checking on the aromas coming from the kitchen when they are baking. They can be frozen and reheated prior to serving." ~ Innkeeper, Smithfield Farm Bed & Breakfast

Dough:
3½   cups all-purpose flour
1   package (2¼ teaspoons) active dry yeast
1¼   cups milk
¼   cup sugar
½   stick butter
1   teaspoon salt
1   large egg

Cinnamon filling:
½   cup sugar
2   teaspoons cinnamon
½   stick butter, melted
½   cup raisins
2   large eggs or egg whites, beaten

For the dough: Combine flour and yeast in a large bowl. Heat milk, sugar, butter and salt until butter is melted and mixture is warm; stir, then add to flour mixture. Add egg and beat for 3 minutes with a mixer at high speed. Form dough into 2 small balls. Put dough in a greased bowl, turning dough once to grease all surfaces. Cover and let rise in a warm place until doubled in size, about 90 minutes. On a lightly floured surface, roll each dough ball into a 16x8-inch rectangle.

For the filling: Preheat oven to 375°F. Mix sugar, cinnamon and melted butter; spread over dough. Sprinkle with raisins (soak raisins in rum first, if desired). Roll up dough jelly-roll style, starting with the long edge. Cut dough into 1-inch slices and place on a greased baking sheet. Brush tops of rolls with beaten egg or egg white. Cover and let rise in warm place until doubled in size, about 30 minutes. Bake for 20 minutes. Serve warm.

ColumnWood

The ColumnWood Bed & Breakfast is centrally located within a two-hour drive of some of the nation's most popular tourist attractions. It is situated in the quiet elegance of historic Bowling Green, settled in 1667.

Four of the six fireplaces still bear their original tiles and coal grates, and several have decorative columns. These columns, along with the columns on both the front and back porches, and the property's huge sycamore trees, some of which are thought to have been planted before the Civil War, inspired the name "ColumnWood."

INNKEEPERS:	Patrick A. DeCrane & Michael E. Thomas
ADDRESS:	233 North Main Street
	Bowling Green, Virginia 22427
TELEPHONE:	(804) 633-5606; (866) 633-9314
E-MAIL:	patmike@bealenet.com
WEBSITE:	www.ColumnWood.com
ROOMS:	4 Rooms; Private baths
CHILDREN:	Children age 15 and older welcome
ANIMALS:	Not allowed; Resident dog
HANDICAPPED:	Not handicapped accessible
DIETARY NEEDS:	Will accommodate guests' special dietary needs

Danish Kuchen

Makes 15 Servings

"When I was a small boy, my father owned a butcher shop on the west side of Cleveland, Ohio. Often, his customers would bring in homemade pastries and give him the recipe. This is one of the best. It is great for serving a large group of people." ~ Innkeeper, ColumnWood Bed & Breakfast

3   cups all-purpose flour
2   teaspoons baking powder
1   cup sugar
½   teaspoon salt
1   cup shortening
3   eggs
2   (18-ounce) cans pie filling (use 2 different flavors such as apple, cherry, blueberry, strawberry, etc.)
Powdered sugar, for dusting

Preheat oven to 350°F. Combine flour, baking powder, sugar, salt and shortening with a pastry blender or 2 knives (as for a pie crust). Add eggs and combine well. Form part of dough into a baseball-size ball and set aside. Roll out remining dough (to about 10x15-inches) and fit into a rimmed baking sheet. Spread 1 type of pie filling on half of each side of dough. Roll out set aside ball of dough and cut into strips. Lay strips in a criss-cross pattern on top of filling. Bake for 30-45 minutes, until golden brown. Cool kuchen, then dust with powdered sugar. Slice and serve.

West Manor

The Summer Kitchen at West Manor offers you complete privacy with the modern comforts of a lovely, restored cottage. The cozy English Country Cottage, built in 1840, originally served as West Manor's summer kitchen. Enjoy the main sleeping area furnished with a wrought-iron bed and completed by a crackling fire.

The inn is close to the Blue Ridge Parkway, National Historical Park at Appomattox, vineyards with wine tasting tours, antique shopping, Smith Mountain Lake, the D-Day Memorial and several colleges.

INNKEEPERS:	Sharon & Greg Lester
ADDRESS:	3594 Elkton Farm Road
	Forest, Virginia 24551
TELEPHONE:	(434) 525-0923
E-MAIL:	info@westmanorbb.com
WEBSITE:	www.westmanorbb.com
ROOMS:	8 Rooms; Private baths
CHILDREN:	Children age 12 and older welcome
ANIMALS:	Not allowed
HANDICAPPED:	Not handicapped accessible
DIETARY NEEDS:	Will accommodate guests' special dietary needs

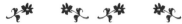

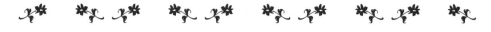

Jam Scones

Makes 12 Scones

2   cups all-purpose flour
¼   cup sugar
2   teaspoons baking powder
½   teaspoon baking soda
¼   teaspoon salt
3   tablespoons butter or margarine, chilled and cut into small pieces
1   (8-ounce) carton low-fat vanilla yogurt
¼-½ cup strawberry or raspberry jam
2   tablespoon chopped pecans

Preheat oven to 400°F. Combine flour, sugar, baking powder, baking soda and salt. Cut in butter with a pastry blender or 2 forks. Add yogurt and stir until moistened. Put dough on a floured board and knead 4-5 times. Pat dough into 2 (8-inch) circles on a greased baking sheet. Cut each circle into 6 wedges. Make a small slit in each wedge and put 1-2 teaspoons of jam in each slit. Sprinkle with pecans. Bake for 13 minutes. Serve warm.

The Foxfield Inn

The Foxfield Inn is located in one of Charlottesville's most picturesque country settings near Foxfield steeplechase track, yet it's only seven miles from downtown Charlottesville. Discriminating B&B guests and newcomers alike will enjoy the ambiance and romance of a country inn at the Foxfield Inn – from sipping fine Virginia wines fireside to relaxing in the soothing hot tub and in-room Jacuzzis.

The inn is designed to offer many common areas for guests inside and outdoors, along with complete privacy in the guest wing.

INNKEEPERS:	Mary Pat & John Hulbert
ADDRESS:	2280 Garth Road
	Charlottesville, Virginia 22901
TELEPHONE:	(434) 923-8892; (866) 369-3536
E-MAIL:	info@foxfield-inn.com
WEBSITE:	www.foxfield-inn.com
ROOMS:	5 Rooms; Private baths
CHILDREN:	Children age 14 and older welcome
ANIMALS:	Not allowed
HANDICAPPED:	Handicapped accessible
DIETARY NEEDS:	Will accommodate guests' special dietary needs

Cinnamon Raisin Scones

Makes 12 Servings

2   cups all-purpose flour
¼   cup sugar
¼   teaspoon salt
1   tablespoon baking powder
1-2   teaspoons cinnamon
5⅓   tablespoons butter, chilled
½   cup raisins
1   cup whipping cream

Preheat oven to 375°F. In a large bowl, combine flour, sugar, salt, baking powder and cinnamon. Cut in butter until mixture resembles a very coarse meal. Stir in raisins. Add whipping cream and stir just until moistened.

Knead dough 5-6 times on a lightly floured surface. Roll out dough ½-inch thick. Cut dough into 2-inch rounds with a biscuit cutter or a glass. Bake for 15 minutes on a lightly greased baking sheet.

Ivy Creek Farm

I vy Creek Farm Bed & Breakfast graces eight acres of country quiet with magnificent views of the Blue Ridge Mountains and Shenandoah Valley. Located in the prestigious Boonsboro area, the inn is just minutes from historic downtown Lynchburg – chartered by Quaker John Lynch in 1786.

The breakfast menu changes daily with house specialties such as eggs with prosciutto, Brie and herbs baked in brioche, cream biscuits with caramel syrup, honey ginger baked pears or other seasonal fruits and fresh baked goods. Complimentary wine, tea and refreshments are offered daily.

INNKEEPERS:	Marilyn & Lynn Brooks
ADDRESS:	2812 Link Road
	Lynchburg, Virginia 24503
TELEPHONE:	(434) 384-3802; (800) 689-7404
E-MAIL:	info@ivycreekfarm.com
WEBSITE:	www.ivycreekfarm.com
ROOMS:	2 Rooms; 1 Suite; Private baths
CHILDREN:	Children age 12 and older welcome
ANIMALS:	Not allowed; Resident dog
HANDICAPPED:	Not handicapped accessible
DIETARY NEEDS:	Will accommodate guests' special dietary needs

Ivy Creek Granola

Makes 10 Cups

"This granola is delicious and is pretty served as a parfait with layers of granola, Greek or plain yogurt, honey and fresh fruit. You can substitute raisins, golden raisins or dates for any of the fruit." ~ Innkeeper, Ivy Creek Farm

3	cups old-fashioned rolled oats
1	cup barley flakes
2	cups sweetened shredded coconut
1	cup sliced almonds
⅓	cup honey, warmed slightly (aids mixing)
¾	cup canola oil
1	cup hazelnuts
1	cup cashews
1½	cups diced dried apricots
1	cup diced figs or dates
1	cup dried cherries
1	cup dried cranberries

Preheat oven to 375°F. In a large bowl, mix oats, barley flakes, coconut and almonds. In a small bowl, mix honey and oil; pour over oat mixture and stir to coat. Spread oat mixture on an ungreased rimmed baking sheet. Bake for 30-35 minutes, stirring every 5-10 minutes, until mixture is evenly golden brown.

While granola is baking, toast cashews and hazelnuts in separate pans for 5-10 minutes, until lightly browned (watch carefully). Wrap hazelnuts in a towel to steam for 10 minutes then remove as much of the bitter skins as possible. Remove oat mixture from oven. Add nuts to oat mixture and set aside to cool (stir mixture occasionally as it cools to keep it from clumping – if you prefer small clusters of granola, stir less frequently).

Combine dried fruits. Store dried fruits and oat mixtures separately until ready to serve so fruit doesn't harden and baked mixture doesn't get soft. Stir in fruit when ready to serve. Stored separately in air-tight containers, the mixtures will keep for at least 2 weeks.

Bennett House

A warm welcome awaits you at the Bennett House Bed & Breakfast. Located in the historic district of Old Town Manassas, the inn is the perfect place for a couple to spend a very special weekend. This Victorian country inn offers many elegant reminders Virginia's genteel past.

The inn is within an hour of Washington, D.C. and is also an easy drive to seven Civil War battlefields. Activities include horse races, boating, cycling, golfing, touring Manassas or just relaxing – whatever suits your fancy.

INNKEEPERS:	Jean & Curtis Harrover
ADDRESS:	9252 Bennett Drive
	Manassas, Virginia 20110
TELEPHONE:	(703) 368-6121; (800) 354-7060
E-MAIL:	jharrover@aol.com
WEBSITE:	www.virginia-bennetthouse.com
ROOMS:	2 Rooms; Private baths
CHILDREN:	Children age 5 and older welcome
ANIMALS:	Not allowed; Resident pets
HANDICAPPED:	Not handicapped accessible
DIETARY NEEDS:	Will accommodate guests' special dietary needs

Apple Cinnamon Oatmeal Casserole

Makes 4 Servings

"This dish is loved by low-cal eaters. Skim milk may be used along with sugar and salt substitutes. The casserole may be prepared the day before and reheated"
~ Innkeeper, Bennett House Bed & Breakfast

2	cups milk or half & half
¼	cup packed brown sugar
1	tablespoon butter
½	teaspoon salt
1	cup quick-cooking oats
2	tablespoons cinnamon (optional)
1	cup chopped peeled apple (optional)
½	cup chopped nuts (optional)
½	cup raisins (optional)

Preheat oven to 350°F. Grease a medium casserole dish. Combine milk, brown sugar, butter and salt in a heavy saucepan over medium heat. Bring to a simmer, cooking until butter is melted and combined, then remove from heat. Put oats in casserole. Stir in milk mixture, cinnamon, apple, nuts and raisins. Bake for 20-30 minutes.

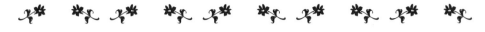

Winterham Plantation

W interham Plantation is a beautifully restored Italianate antebellum mansion, with the elegance of Virginia's historic grandeur and the convenience of modern amenities.

Winterham Plantation Tours offers the ultimate Civil War tour. The last major battle of the war was fought in Amelia County, at Little Sayler's Creek, now known as Sailor's Creek Battlefield. General Robert E. Lee lost eight generals and a quarter of his troops. When this engagement was over, both sides knew the end of the war was near.

INNKEEPERS:	Gayle Carden Hudert
ADDRESS:	11441 Grub Hill Church Road
	Amelia Court House, Virginia 23002
TELEPHONE:	(804) 561-4519; (866) 561-4519
E-MAIL:	stay@winterham.com
WEBSITE:	www.winterham.com
ROOMS:	2 Rooms; 2 Suites; Private baths
CHILDREN:	Welcome
ANIMALS:	Not allowed; Resident dog
HANDICAPPED:	Not handicapped accessible
DIETARY NEEDS:	Will accommodate guests' special dietary needs

Easy Baked Oatmeal Squares

Makes 12 Squares

"Here's an easy way to add oatmeal to your breakfast. My baked adaptation is somewhere between a bowl of oatmeal and a cookie. It's healthy and delicious, even when re-heated." ~ Innkeeper, Winterham Plantation Bed & Breakfast

4   cups old-fashioned rolled oats
1   teaspoon baking powder
1   teaspoon salt
1   stick butter, softened
½   cup packed brown sugar
2   eggs
2   cups milk
Fried apples, for serving (optional)

Preheat oven to 350°F. In a large bowl, combine oats, baking powder and salt. Add butter and mix well. In a small bowl, beat eggs and milk; add to oats mixture and stir well. Pour mixture into a greased 7x11-inch glass baking dish. Bake for about 20 minutes, or until set in center and edges are brown. Cut into 12 squares and serve warm with fried apples, if desired.

Williamsburg Sampler

The Williamsburg Sampler Bed & Breakfast Inn is a fine, 18th-century plantation-style Colonial home. The inn is located in Williamsburg's Architectural Corridor Protection District. Although the home was built in 1976, it captures the early American spirit of Colonial Williamsburg. You will love its warm atmosphere, tasteful décor and fine craftsmanship.

The Williamsburg Sampler was officially proclaimed by Virginia's governor as "Inn of the Year in the Commonwealth of Virginia."

INNKEEPERS:	Ike Sisane
ADDRESS:	922 Jamestown Road
	Williamsburg, Virginia 23185
TELEPHONE:	(757) 253-0398; (800) 722-1169
E-MAIL:	info@williamsburgsampler.com
WEBSITE:	www.williamsburgsampler.com
ROOMS:	2 Rooms; 2 Suites; Private baths
CHILDREN:	Children age 12 and older welcome
ANIMALS:	Not allowed
HANDICAPPED:	Not handicapped accessible
DIETARY NEEDS:	Will accommodate guests' special dietary needs

Skip Lunch for Dessert

Makes 4 to 5 Servings

⅓   cup old-fashioned rolled oats
1   cup heavy cream
3   tablespoons powdered sugar
3   teaspoons dark rum

Preheat oven to 400°F. Chill individual serving parfait glasses. Chill a large bowl. Spread oats in a 9-inch round cake pan or an 8x8-inch baking pan. Bake oats for about 15 minutes, shaking pan occasionally, until oats are a rich, golden brown (watch carefully for signs of burning and adjust oven temperature or baking time accordingly). Remove oats from oven and cool.

In the chilled bowl, whip cream with a mixer at high speed until it begins to thicken. Add sugar and beat until cream is firm enough to form unwavering peaks on beaters when lifted out of bowl. Gently stir in rum, 1 teaspoon at a time. With a rubber spatula, gently fold in toasted oats with an "over/under" cutting motion (rather than a stirring motion). Pile cream into chilled parfait glasses and serve immediately.

Pancakes & Waffles

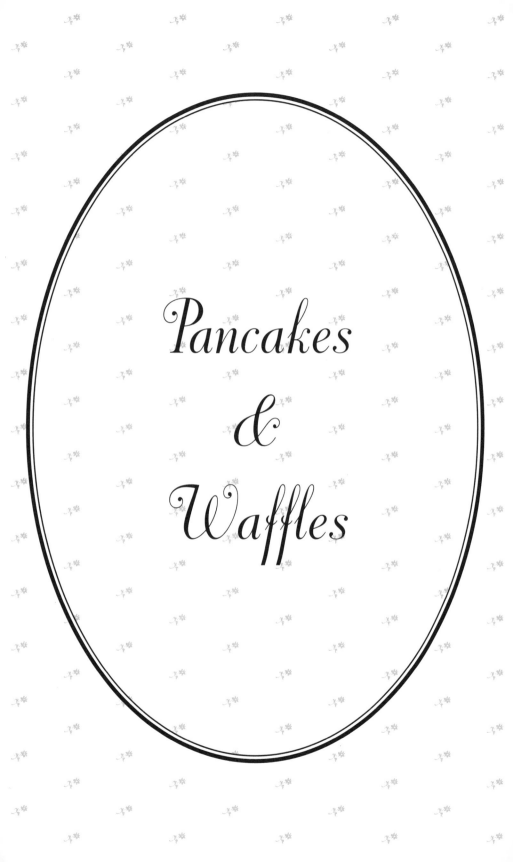

Pancakes
&
Waffles

Colonial Gardens

The Colonial Gardens Bed & Breakfast is ideally located near Colonial Williamsburg and the College of William & Mary. It is the closest Williamsburg inn to the Jamestown Settlement. The inn is situated near the Williamsburg Winery and is just minutes from Busch Gardens, Water Country USA, the Williamsburg Antique Mall and more than 20 world-class golf courses.

"Your home and hospitality provided just the retreat we desired … we were pampered!" ~ Guests, Indiana

INNKEEPERS:	Scottie & Wil Phillips
ADDRESS:	1109 Jamestown Road
	Williamsburg, Virginia 23185
TELEPHONE:	(757) 220-8087; (800) 886-9715
E-MAIL:	colgdns@widomaker.com
WEBSITE:	www.colonial-gardens.com
ROOMS:	4 Rooms; 2 Suites; Private baths
CHILDREN:	Children age 14 and older welcome
ANIMALS:	Not allowed
HANDICAPPED:	Not handicapped accessible
DIETARY NEEDS:	Will accommodate guests' special dietary needs

Gingerbread Pancakes with Orange Marmalade Syrup

Makes 4 Servings

3   cups buttermilk pancake mix
3   tablespoons sugar
3   tablespoons cinnamon
1¼   teaspoons allspice
½   teaspoon ground ginger
½   teaspoon nutmeg
½   teaspoon ground cloves
2½   cups water

Orange marmalade syrup:
⅔   cup pure maple syrup
⅓   cup orange marmalade

Combine pancake mix, sugar, cinnamon, allspice, ginger, nutmeg and cloves; make a well in center of mixture. Add water to well and stir just until dry ingredients are moistened (if mixture is too thick, add more water or milk, as needed). Spoon about 2 tablespoons of batter per pancake onto a hot, lightly greased griddle or skillet. Cook pancakes until browned on each side. Serve with warm orange marmalade syrup.

For the orange marmalade syrup: Combine maple syrup and marmalade in a small saucepan over medium heat. Bring to a boil, stirring constantly, lower heat and simmer until marmalade is melted and combined. Remove from heat. Serve warm.

By the Side of the Road

By the Side of the Road Bed & Breakfast is located within minutes of the Blue Ridge Parkway and Skyline Drive, the American Museum of Frontier Culture, Massanutten Mountains and the Old Order Amish Market. Also nearby are the Staunton and Lexington historic districts, three colleges, antique malls and shops, Civil War landmarks and museums, Luray and Shenandoah Caverns, restaurants, theaters, wineries and more.

Voted by inngoers in *Arrington's Bed & Breakfast Journal's Book of Lists* as "one of the Top 15 bed & breakfasts in the U.S. near a college or university."

INNKEEPERS:	Janice & Dennis Fitzgerald
ADDRESS:	491 Garbers Church Road
	Harrisonburg, Virginia 22801
TELEPHONE:	(540) 801-0430
E-MAIL:	stay@bythesideoftheroad.com
WEBSITE:	www.bythesideoftheroad.com
ROOMS:	4 Suites; 1 Cottage; Private baths
CHILDREN:	Welcome
ANIMALS:	Not allowed; Resident dog
HANDICAPPED:	Not handicapped accessible
DIETARY NEEDS:	Will accommodate guests' special dietary needs

Buttermilk Pecan Pancakes with Brown Sugar Butter Sauce

Makes 4 to 6 Servings

"One morning, a guest called me to the table to whisper in my ear, 'These are the best pancakes I have ever tasted, but don't tell my mother!'" - Innkeeper, By the Side of the Road Bed & Breakfast

3   large eggs, separated
1⅔   cups buttermilk
3   tablespoons butter, melted
1½   cups all-purpose flour
1   teaspoon baking soda
1   teaspoon baking powder
½   teaspoon salt
1   cup chopped pecans plus extra for topping

Brown sugar butter sauce:
½   stick butter
1   cup packed light brown sugar
1   cup half & half, warmed

In a small bowl, combine egg yolks, buttermilk and butter. Sift together flour, baking soda, baking powder and salt into a large bowl. Add egg yolk mixture to flour mixture and mix lightly. In a clean bowl, beat egg whites until stiff, but not dry. Gently fold egg whites and pecans into batter. Using about ¼ cup of batter per pancake, cook pancakes on a non-stick or lightly greased griddle or skillet until golden brown on each side. Top pancakes with warm brown sugar butter. Sprinkle with chopped pecans and serve.

For the brown sugar butter sauce: Combine butter and brown sugar in a small saucepan over low heat. Gently stir in warm half & half. Stirring constantly, bring to a low boil. Process in a food processor or blender for 30 seconds (or whisk sauce with a wire whisk for 30 seconds). Serve warm.

Strathmore House on the Shenandoah

Put aside rush hour traffic and the banality of television and revel in the serenity of English gardens, a rocking chair on the Strathmore House's wraparound porch, or a leisurely walk over four acres of landscaped grounds for a bird's-eye view of the Meems Bottom Covered Bridge (one of only a few covered bridges left in Virginia). The inn is located on the banks of the Shenandoah River, adjacent to the covered bridge.

Four posters, crown canopies and feather beds are just a few of the special touches that reflect the innkeepers' attention to detail and guest comfort.

INNKEEPERS:	Kay & Jim Payne
ADDRESS:	658 Wissler Road
	Mt. Jackson, Virginia 22842
TELEPHONE:	(540) 477-4141; (888) 921-6139
E-MAIL:	strath@shentel.net
WEBSITE:	www.strathmorehouse.com
ROOMS:	4 Rooms; Private baths
CHILDREN:	Not allowed
ANIMALS:	Not allowed; Resident cat
HANDICAPPED:	Not handicapped accessible
DIETARY NEEDS:	Will accommodate guests' special dietary needs

Toasted Coconut Hot Cakes with Pineapple Mango Sauce

Makes 4 Servings

Pineapple mango sauce:
½   fresh golden pineapple, cut into small cubes
1   ripe mango, cut into small cubes
2   teaspoons Cointreau or other orange liqueur (or orange juice)

Toasted coconut hot cakes:
2   cups all-purpose flour
4   tablespoons sugar
½   teaspoon salt
2   teaspoons baking power
1   teaspoon baking soda
2   eggs
2   cups buttermilk
½   teaspoon pure coconut extract
½   stick unsalted butter, melted
½-1 cup coconut, toasted
Sweetened whipped cream mixed with a dollop of golden rum

For the pineapple mango sauce: Combine pineapple and mango. Stir in Cointreau and let stand for 30 minutes to marinate.

For the hot cakes: In a medium bowl, lightly mix flour, sugar, salt, baking powder and baking soda. In a large bowl, beat eggs with a mixer until frothy. Beat in buttermilk and coconut extract. Beat in flour mixture, then melted butter, beating just until mixture is smooth (do not overbeat).

Heat griddle to high heat (about 350°F on an electric griddle). Pour batter by ½-cupsful onto griddle. Sprinkle each hot cake with 1 tablespoon of toasted coconut. Cook for about 2 minutes per side. Serve with sweetened whipped cream and pineapple mango sauce.

The Widow Kip's Country Inn

The Widow Kip's Country Inn is a restored 1830 Victorian homestead. The inn is nestled on seven rural acres with a bird's-eye view of the Shenandoah River just 50 yards away. Many splendors of the Shenandoah Valley, including George Washington & Jefferson National Forest and the Massanutten Mountains, are within minutes of this serene hideaway.

Enjoy the inn's pool and bicycles, nearby horseback-riding, golf, skiing, hiking, fishing, caverns, canoeing, hot air ballooning, Civil War battlefields and museums and wineries at this four-season inn.

INNKEEPERS:	Betty & Bob Luse
ADDRESS:	355 Orchard Drive
	Mt. Jackson, Virginia 22842
TELEPHONE:	(540) 477-2400; (800) 478-8714
E-MAIL:	widokips@shentel.net
WEBSITE:	www.widowkips.com
ROOMS:	5 Rooms; 2 Cottages; Private baths
CHILDREN:	Welcome
ANIMALS:	Dogs & cats welcome; Resident outdoor cat
HANDICAPPED:	Not handicapped accessible
DIETARY NEEDS:	Will accommodate guests' special dietary needs

Apple Crisp Pancakes with Apple Cinnamon Syrup

Makes 4 Servings

1	egg, beaten
¾	cup milk
1	teaspoon vanilla
2½	cups pancake mix, divided
¾	cup chunky applesauce plus extra for serving
½	cup quick cooking oats
¼	cup packed brown sugar
2	tablespoons butter, softened

Apple cinnamon syrup:

1	cup sugar
2	tablespoons cornstarch
2	teaspoons cinnamon
2	cups apple cider or natural apple juice
2	tablespoons lemon juice
½	stick butter

Preheat oven to 375°F. Spray a baking pan with non-stick cooking spray. In a large bowl, combine egg, milk, vanilla, 2 cups of pancake mix and ¾ cup of applesauce. Spread mixture in pan. In a medium bowl, combine oats, brown sugar, remaining ½ cup of pancake mix and butter. Sprinkle oats mixture over ingredients in pan. Bake for 14-16 minutes. Serve with applesauce and warm apple cinnamon syrup.

For the apple cinnamon syrup: Combine sugar, cornstarch, cinnamon, apple cider and lemon juice in a medium saucepan over medium heat. Bring to a boil, then remove pan from heat and stir in butter until melted and combined. Serve warm.

The Mountain Rose Inn

N estled along the banks of Rock Castle Creek in Woolwine, the Mountain Rose Inn offers historical country elegance in the shadows of the Blue Ridge Mountains. Secluded on 100 acres, the inn is the perfect place to enjoy strolling the lawns and gardens.

Guests can also visit the Chateau Morrisette and Villa Appalachia wineries, fish along the banks of the creek, enjoy local bluegrass music, take a dip in the inn's pool, tour the Blue Ridge Parkway or, as many of the inn's guests prefer, luxuriate in the fine art of doing nothing!

INNKEEPERS:	Reeves & Melodie Pogue
ADDRESS:	1787 Charity Highway
	Woolwine, Virginia 24185
TELEPHONE:	(276) 930-1057
E-MAIL:	info@mountainrose-inn.com
WEBSITE:	www.mountainrose-inn.com
ROOMS:	5 Rooms; Private baths
CHILDREN:	Children age 2 and older welcome
ANIMALS:	Not allowed
HANDICAPPED:	Call ahead
DIETARY NEEDS:	Call ahead

Pumpkin Pancakes

Makes 10 Servings

"Every fall our local volunteer fire department has an apple butter festival. They start peeling thousands of apples on a Thursday night and continue working until Saturday when they cook the apple butter outside in huge kettles. Saturday afternoon the apple butter is canned while in the background local musicians play bluegrass, dancers flat foot and barbecue is served. The festival has become so popular that there is now a limit on how many quarts of apple butter one may buy. We serve our apple butter on these special pancakes for a late fall treat!" ~ Innkeeper, The Mountain Rose Inn

3   cups Bisquick
1½   tablespoons packed brown sugar
1   tablespoon cinnamon
1½   teaspoons allspice
2   cups milk
3   tablespoons vegetable oil
3   large eggs
¾   cup canned pumpkin
1   teaspoon vanilla extract
Apple butter, for serving

In a large bowl, combine Bisquick, brown sugar, cinnamon and allspice. Add milk, oil, eggs, pumpkin and vanilla; stir until smooth. Pour ¼ cup of batter per pancake onto a hot greased griddle or skillet. Cook pancakes until browned on each side. Serve with apple butter.

Ivy Creek Farm

I vy Creek Farm Bed & Breakfast began as a modest cottage built around 1840 on land purchased from Major Samuel Scott's plantation. Several additions and improvements have been added over the years. The old barn stands as a reminder of the farm's use in the early 20th century as a 120-acre dairy farm known as "Stokes Ivy Creek Farm."

Share the innkeepers' love of antiques, good reading, fine music, history, nature, art, conviviality and fine food and wine. Or, swim in the beautiful indoor heated swimming pool and relax in the adjoining whirlpool spa.

INNKEEPERS:	Marilyn & Lynn Brooks
ADDRESS:	2812 Link Road
	Lynchburg, Virginia 24503
TELEPHONE:	(434) 384-3802; (800) 689-7404
E-MAIL:	info@ivycreekfarm.com
WEBSITE:	www.ivycreekfarm.com
ROOMS:	2 Rooms; 1 Suite; Private baths
CHILDREN:	Children age 12 and older welcome
ANIMALS:	Not allowed; Resident dog
HANDICAPPED:	Not handicapped accessible
DIETARY NEEDS:	Will accommodate guests' special dietary needs

Lemon Soufflé Pancakes

Makes 4 Servings

1	cup plus 2 tablespoons all-purpose flour
3	tablespoons sugar, divided
1½	teaspoons baking powder
½	teaspoon salt
¼	teaspoon nutmeg

Grated zest of 5 lemons

¾	stick unsalted butter, melted and kept warm
¾	cup ricotta cheese
¼	cup plus 2 tablespoons buttermilk
2	tablespoons fresh lemon juice
¾	teaspoon vanilla extract
3	large eggs, separated

Raspberry syrup, for serving
Powdered sugar, for garnish
Fresh mint sprigs, for garnish

In a large bowl, combine flour, 1 tablespoon of sugar, baking powder, salt, nutmeg and lemon zest. In a small bowl, combine butter, ricotta cheese, buttermilk, lemon juice, vanilla and egg yolks; whisk until smooth. Add egg yolk mixture to flour mixture and whisk until smooth (the batter will be quite dense).

In a bowl, beat egg whites with a mixer at medium speed until soft peaks form. Sprinkle in remaining 2 tablespoons of sugar and continue beating until stiff peaks form. With a rubber spatula, carefully fold egg whites into batter, ¼ at a time (batter need not be completely uniform – a few streaks of egg white are fine). Cover and refrigerate for up to 1 hour.

Lightly coat a griddle or a large non-stick skillet with non-stick cooking spray and preheat over medium heat. Pour ¾-cup of batter per pancake into skillet (do not crowd pan). Cook pancakes until golden brown on each side. Top pancakes with raspberry syrup. Sprinkle with powdered sugar and garnish with mint sprigs to serve.

Afton Mountain

Whether you're touring the scenic Blue Ridge Parkway or Skyline Drive, visiting central Virginia's award-winning wineries or getting away for a weekend of golf or skiing, the Afton Mountain Bed & Breakfast is an ideal choice. After a day of sightseeing, hiking or wine tasting, take a relaxing swim in the pool, enjoy fresh-baked cookies or catch up on your reading on one of the large porches.

This 1848 Victorian farmhouse in the foothills of the Blue Ridge Mountains features antiques, a stained-glass entrance way and original heart-pine floors.

INNKEEPERS:	Orquida & Dan Ingraham
ADDRESS:	10273 Rockfish Valley Highway
	Afton, Virginia 22920
TELEPHONE:	(540) 456-6844; (800) 769-6844
E-MAIL:	aftonmountain@yahoo.com
WEBSITE:	www.aftonmountain.com
ROOMS:	5 Rooms; Private baths
CHILDREN:	Welcome
ANIMALS:	Not allowed; Resident dog
HANDICAPPED:	Not handicapped accessible
DIETARY NEEDS:	Will accommodate guests' special dietary needs

Lemon Pancakes with Fresh Fruit

Makes 4 Servings

"This recipe was inspired by a wonderful breakfast we had at Crystal Springs Bed & Breakfast in Killarney, Ireland. It makes a beautiful presentation." - Innkeeper, Afton Mountain Bed & Breakfast

Favorite buttermilk pancake recipe (see page 61)
1 teaspoon grated lemon zest
1 mango, peeled and chopped
2 kiwis, peeled and chopped
1 cup grapes, cut in half
1 apple, chopped
1 pear, chopped
½ cup blueberries
½ cup raspberries
5 tablespoons Lyle's Golden Syrup*
1 (10-ounce) jar Dickinson's Lemon Curd*
Whipped cream, for serving

Prepare pancake batter. Stir in lemon zest. Combine fruit in a large bowl; set aside. Combine golden syrup with 3 tablespoons lemon curd; heat in microwave until bubbly, then stir to combine and set aside.

Pour ¾ cup of batter onto a greased griddle or skillet over medium heat to form 1 large pancake (about 8-inches in diameter). Cook until golden on each side. Turn pancake onto a plate top-side-down for 30 seconds to steam it, then turn pancake over and spread with 2-3 tablespoons of lemon curd. Roll up pancake, jelly roll-style, and place seam-side-down on a serving plate. Repeat with remaining batter to make 4 pancakes.

Microwave golden syrup mixture for 30 seconds to warm it. Place 1 cup of fruit beside each pancake. Drizzle 2 tablespoons of golden syrup mixture over each pancake. Garnish with 3 dollops of whipped cream and serve.

*Note: Lyle's Golden Syrup is a sweet syrup from England. It is used like maple syrup. Lyle's Golden Syrup and Dickinson's Lemon Curd are available at some larger groceries and specialty food stores.

The Buchanan Inn

The Buchanan Inn at the Green Grove Station was built around 1915 to accommodate the growing family of William and Mary Buchanan. Mr. Buck (as he was called) had come to the area as a school teacher and married the local postmistress, Mary Hart.

The old house provided lodging for numerous school teachers over the years and Mary kept her fledgling teenage daughters (and anyone in sight) busy putting together lunches for the Norfolk and Western passengers and crew traveling from Abingdon to North Carolina.

INNKEEPERS:	Annette & Jim Goode
ADDRESS:	41261 Green Cove Road
	Damascus, Virginia 24236
TELEPHONE:	(276) 388-3367; (877) 300-9328
E-MAIL:	buchananinn@aol.com
WEBSITE:	www.thebuchananinn.com
ROOMS:	3 Rooms; Private baths
CHILDREN:	Welcome
ANIMALS:	Not allowed
HANDICAPPED:	Not handicapped accessible
DIETARY NEEDS:	Will accommodate guests' special dietary needs

Baked Apple Pancake

Makes 1 to 2 Servings

"This recipe was given to us by our friend, Joyce Luffman, a gourmet cook!"
~ Innkeeper, The Buchanan Inn at the Green Cove Station

½ stick butter
⅓ cup packed brown sugar
1 medium Golden Delicious apple, peeled and thinly sliced
1 cup pancake mix
⅔ cup milk
2 tablespoons vegetable oil
1 large egg, beaten
Maple syrup, for serving

Preheat oven to 350°F. Melt butter in an 8-inch cast-iron skillet (or other oven-proof skillet) over medium-low heat. Add brown sugar and apples; cook until sugar is dissolved, gently stirring apples to coat.

Combine pancake mix, milk, oil and egg; pour over apple mixture in skillet. Raise heat to medium and cook until bubbles form on top of pancake. Transfer skillet to oven and bake for 12-17 minutes, until golden brown. Invert skillet over a serving platter and remove pancake. Serve with maple syrup and bacon or sausage.

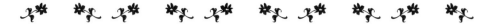

Newport House

N ewport House Bed & Breakfast is Williamsburg's most historically authentic bed & breakfast. It was built to museum standards in 1988 from a 1756 design by famed architect Peter Harrison. The house on which the Newport House was based was the Banister Plantation near Newport, Rhode Island, which was demolished in 1976 to make way for a carpark.

Newport House Bed & Breakfast is furnished with period English and American antiques and reproductions (over a dozen of which were designed by Harrison, who was also Colonial America's top furniture designer).

INNKEEPERS:	John & Cathy Millar
ADDRESS:	710 South Henry Street
	Williamsburg, Virginia 23185
TELEPHONE:	(757) 229-1775; (877) 565-1775
E-MAIL:	info@newporthousebb.com
WEBSITE:	www.newporthousebb.com
ROOMS:	2 Rooms; Private baths
CHILDREN:	Welcome
ANIMALS:	Not allowed; Resident rabbit
HANDICAPPED:	Not handicapped accessible
DIETARY NEEDS:	Will accommodate guests' special dietary needs

Colonial Jonnycakes

Makes 4 to 6 Servings

"George Washington considered that he had not breakfasted if he had not had jonnycakes. The rum is included in the recipe because it was the primary food preservative in Colonial days for meat, fish, fruit, vegetables and flour. The name 'jonnycake' – with no 'h' – is short for 'journeycake.'" ~ Innkeeper, Newport House Bed & Breakfast

2	cups white flint cornmeal*
2	cups dark rum (Black Seal from Bermuda is the best)
¼	cup milk or half & half
1	teaspoon salt
1	tablespoon sugar
1	tablespoon molasses

Hot water

Preheat a greased griddle to 400°F or a skillet over medium heat. In a bowl, combine all ingredients, except hot water; let stand for 10 minutes. Stir in enough hot water to form consistency of runny mashed potatoes.

Drop batter by tablespoonsful onto griddle. Cook jonnycakes for about 90 seconds per side. Serve with butter and molasses (or something else from the Caribbean, such as lime curd, pineapple preserves, guava jelly or banana or nutmeg jam).

*Note: The best source for white flint cornmeal, the authentic jonnycake meal, is Carpenter's Grist Mill ~ (401) 783-5483.

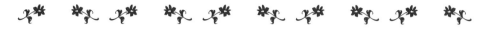

Applewood Inn

B reakfast at the Applewood Inn consists of fresh in-season fruit (from the inn's garden when possible), whole-grain breads or muffins and entrées such as gingered peach soufflé, omelets, whole grain pancakes and breakfast meats. Jams and jellies are made on premises and are available for sale. The emphasis is on hearty and delicious, but healthy breakfasts.

Adjoining the inn property are more than 900 acres of forest and meadow criss-crossed with miles of trails for hiking, riding (bring your own horses) and llama treks (two hour guided hikes leading one of the inn's llamas).

INNKEEPERS:	Linda & Christian Best
ADDRESS:	Tarn Beck Lane off Buffalo Bend Road
	Lexington, Virginia 24450
TELEPHONE:	(540) 463-1962; (800) 463-1902
E-MAIL:	inn@applewoodbb.com
WEBSITE:	www.applewoodbb.com
ROOMS:	4 Rooms; Private baths
CHILDREN:	Children age 6 and older welcome
ANIMALS:	Dogs allowed in 1 Room; Resident dogs & cat
HANDICAPPED:	Call ahead
DIETARY NEEDS:	Will accommodate guests' special dietary needs

Corn Fritter Pancakes

Makes 4 Servings

"This is a very simple, low-sugar (none added), low-fat (until you add butter and maple syrup), hearty dish. Served with butter or yogurt and maple syrup, it has a nice visual appeal. Before moving to Virginia, we owned an inn in the Berkshires of western Massachusetts, where we grew our own corn. Visitors came back just for these pancakes." ~ Innkeeper, Applewood Inn & Llama Trekking

½	cup all-purpose flour
1½	cups stone-ground yellow cornmeal
1	tablespoon baking powder
½	teaspoon baking soda
¼	teaspoon salt
2	large eggs, beaten
½	cup non-fat or low-fat plain yogurt
¼	cup canola oil
1	(14-ounce) can corn (undrained)
1½	cups buttermilk (use up to 2 cups for thinner pancakes)

Melted butter or yogurt, for serving
Maple syrup, for serving

In a large bowl, combine flour, cornmeal, baking powder, baking soda and salt. In a medium bowl, beat eggs. Stir yogurt, oil, corn (and corn liquid) and buttermilk into eggs. Add egg mixture to flour mixture and stir to combine (do not overmix).

Cook pancakes on a greased, preheated griddle or skillet until edges of pancakes appear dry. Turn and cook other side. Serve with melted butter or a dollop of yogurt and maple syrup.

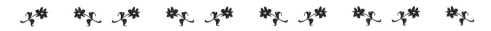

South Court Inn

Experience the glamour and elegance of a "high" Victorian mansion. Located in the heart of the historic Shenandoah Valley, only two hours from Washington, D.C., the charm and elegance of the South Court Inn encourages visitors to slow down, relax and enjoy the slower pace of a bygone era.

Breakfast includes delicious offerings such as compote of fresh fruits *glace*, South Court maple walnut sticky buns, individual cheese soufflés à la South Court and homemade sourdough bread and fruit butters and jams.

INNKEEPERS:	Anita & Tom Potts
ADDRESS:	160 South Court Street
	Luray, Virginia 22835
TELEPHONE:	(540) 843-0980; (888) 749-8055
E-MAIL:	inn@southcourtinn.com
WEBSITE:	www.southcourtinn.com
ROOMS:	3 Rooms; Private baths
CHILDREN:	Children age 12 and older welcome; 1 per room
ANIMALS:	Not allowed
HANDICAPPED:	Not handicapped accessible
DIETARY NEEDS:	Call ahead

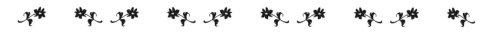

Lemon Belgian Waffles with Homemade Berry Syrup

Makes 8 to 10 Servings

1   cup cake flour or all-purpose flour (cake flour yields crisper waffles)
½   teaspoon salt
1   tablespoon baking powder
½   teaspoon freshly grated nutmeg
1   cup milk or buttermilk
Juice and grated zest of 2 lemons
3   large eggs, separated
½   teaspoon cream or tartar

Homemade berry syrup:
¼   cup water
½   cup light corn syrup
1   cup sugar
1   pound favorite fresh or frozen berries (raspberries are especially good)

Sift together flour, salt, baking powder and nutmeg into a bowl; make a well in center. Mix buttermilk and lemon zest and juice well in a blender or a bowl. Add egg yolks and mix until well incorporated. In a clean bowl, beat egg whites with a mixer at low speed until they begin to froth. Add cream of tartar and beat at high speed until glossy, stiff peaks form. Add milk mixture to well in flour mixture and whisk until no large lumps remain. Gently fold ½ of egg whites into batter, then fold in remaining egg whites (batter will be streaked with egg whites). Bake waffles on a preheated waffle iron to a rich golden brown. Serve immediately topped with warm berry syrup.

For the berry syrup: Bring water and corn syrup to a boil in a saucepan over medium heat. Add sugar and stir to dissolve. Add berries. Lower heat to low and cook gently for about 30 minutes. Serve warm.

Hearth n' Holly Inn

T ake a journey back in time to a simpler, less stressful era. Enjoy the ambiance of a bed & breakfast that combines the beauty and tradition of the 1890s with the comforts and conveniences of the new millennium. Experience the relaxing comforts of pillowtop beds and a cozy fire. Savor the beauty of nature and the marvelous mountain views as you while away the hours on the front porch or in the outdoor spa.

The inn is located on 15 acres with views of Massanutten Mountain, and is just ten minutes from Massanutten Resort and James Madison University.

INNKEEPERS:	Dennis & Doris Brown
ADDRESS:	46 Songbird Lane
	Penn Laird, Virginia 22846
TELEPHONE:	(800) 209-1379
E-MAIL:	hhinn@shentel.net
WEBSITE:	www.hearthnholly.com
ROOMS:	3 Rooms; Private baths
CHILDREN:	Welcome
ANIMALS:	Not allowed; Resident dog & cat
HANDICAPPED:	Not handicapped accessible
DIETARY NEEDS:	Will accommodate guests' special dietary needs

Pumpkin Waffles with Cinnamon Sugar Butter

Makes 4 Servings

"This batter holds up beautifully when made the night before. Leftover batter keeps well in the refrigerator for the next day." ~ Innkeeper, Hearth n' Holly Inn

2¼ cups all-purpose flour
1 tablespoon plus 1 teaspoon baking powder
2 teaspoons cinnamon
1 teaspoon allspice
1 teaspoon ground ginger
½ teaspoon salt
¼ cup packed brown sugar
1 cup canned pumpkin
2 cups milk
4 large eggs, separated
½ stick unsalted butter, melted

Cinnamon sugar butter:
1 stick unsalted butter, softened
2 tablespoons sugar
1 teaspoon cinnamon

Sift together flour, baking powder, cinnamon, allspice, ginger, salt and brown sugar into a large bowl. In a medium bowl, combine pumpkin, milk, egg yolks and melted butter; mix well. Make a well in flour mixture; add pumpkin mixture to well and stir until combined. In a medium, clean, dry bowl beat egg whites until soft peaks form; fold gently into batter just until combined. Bake waffles in a preheated waffle iron until golden brown. Serve with cinnamon sugar butter.

For the cinnamon sugar butter: Warm butter in a small bowl or saucepan until smooth and soft. Add sugar and cinnamon; mix well. If not using immediately, refrigerate, then let stand at room temperature to soften before serving.

South River Country Inn

S outh River Country Inn is located on a 100-acre working farm with panoramic views of the Blue Ridge Mountains. The inn is situated in the heart of the South River Valley, just five minutes from the Skyline Drive. Here you have a unique opportunity to relax and enjoy all the warmth and comforts of life on a farm.

The original Virginia-style farm house has been faithfully restored to preserve its authentic country charm while providing guests with all the amenities of a modern home.

INNKEEPERS:	Judy & Cliff Braun
ADDRESS:	3011 South River Road
	Stanardsville, Virginia 22973
TELEPHONE:	(434) 985-2901; (877) 874-4473
E-MAIL:	cbraun@sprintmail.com
WEBSITE:	www.southrivercountryinn.com
ROOMS:	3 Rooms; 1 Suite; 1 Cottage; Private baths
CHILDREN:	Children age 6 and older welcome
ANIMALS:	Not allowed; Resident outdoor dog
HANDICAPPED:	Not handicapped accessible
DIETARY NEEDS:	Will accommodate guests' special dietary needs

Cinnamon Pecan Waffles

Makes 4 Servings

"Fabulous – well worth the extra steps." ~ Innkeeper, South River Country Inn

1	cup all-purpose flour
1	tablespoon cornmeal
1	teaspoon baking powder
½	teaspoon baking soda
½	teaspoon salt
½	teaspoon sugar
1	teaspoon cinnamon
1½	cups buttermilk
2	large eggs, separated
2	tablespoons vegetable oil

Chopped pecans

Sift together flour, cornmeal, baking powder, baking soda, salt, sugar and cinnamon into a medium bowl. In a large bowl, beat buttermilk, egg yolks and oil. Stir flour mixture into buttermilk mixture. In a clean bowl, beat egg whites until stiff, then gently fold into batter. Pour batter onto a preheated Belgian waffle iron. Sprinkle pecans on top of batter. Bake until golden brown, about 4 minutes.

French Toast, Bread Pudding, Crêpes & Blintzes

French Toast, Bread Pudding, Crêpes & Blintzes

The Inn at Monticello

The Inn at Monticello is located only a mile from Monticello and less than 10 minutes from Charlottesville's historic downtown district, the University of Virginia, restaurants and shopping. A charming country manor home built in the mid-1800s, the inn sits on five landscaped acres at the foot of Thomas Jefferson's own Monticello Mountain.

Breakfast includes home baked breads and muffins and entrées such as French toast with peach apricot sauce, blueberry pancakes smothered with fresh fruit in orange sauce or a Southern favorite – praline French toast.

INNKEEPERS:	Norm & Becky Lindway
ADDRESS:	Route 20 South, 1188 Scottsville Road
	Charlottesville, Virginia 22902
TELEPHONE:	(434) 979-3593
E-MAIL:	stay@innatmonticello.com
WEBSITE:	www.innatmonticello.com
ROOMS:	5 Rooms; 1 Suite; Private baths
CHILDREN:	Children age 12 and older welcome
ANIMALS:	Not allowed; Resident cat
HANDICAPPED:	Not handicapped accessible
DIETARY NEEDS:	Will accommodate guests' special dietary needs

Peaches & Crème Brûlée French Toast

Makes 5 to 10 Servings

Plan ahead, this delicious French toast needs to be started the night before.

1	stick butter
1	cup packed brown sugar
½	cup corn syrup
10	(1-inch-thick) slices bread
6	large eggs
1½	cups half & half
1	teaspoon vanilla extract
1	teaspoon Triple Sec
¼	teaspoon salt
1	pound fresh or frozen (defrosted) peeled, sliced peaches
½	cup white sugar
¼	cup peach brandy

Spray a 10x15-inch baking dish with non-stick cooking spray. Melt butter, brown sugar and corn syrup in a heavy saucepan over medium-low heat. Cook, stirring until smooth, then pour mixture into baking dish. Put bread on top of butter mixture. Whisk together eggs, half & half, vanilla, Triple Sec and salt; pour over bread. Cover and refrigerate overnight.

The next day, let French toast stand at room temperature for 30 minutes. Preheat oven to 350°F. Bake French toast for 30-35 minutes. While French toast is baking, put peaches in a bowl. Add white sugar and peach brandy; stir to combine. Put 1-2 pieces of French toast on each plate, brown sugar-side-up. Top with some peaches to serve.

Inn at 802

The Inn at 802
A Williamsburg Bed & Breakfast

Arrive at the Inn at 802 and your "key to relaxation" awaits you. Offering historic Williamsburg lodging, the inn is in a perfect location, with the College of William & Mary just across the street and Colonial Williamsburg a short 12-minute walk away. In addition, Yorktown, Busch Gardens and the Jamestown Settlement are all a short drive from the inn.

Return to the inn and relax in the common areas. Browse the extensive library, then settle in with a book by the fire, or enjoy the warmth of the sun in the delightfully cheery sun room overlooking the garden and patio area.

INNKEEPERS:	Joe & Cathy Bradley
ADDRESS:	802 Jamestown Road
	Williamsburg, Virginia 23185
TELEPHONE:	(757) 345-3316; (888) 757-3316
E-MAIL:	cathy@innat802.com
WEBSITE:	www.innat802.com
ROOMS:	4 Rooms; Private baths
CHILDREN:	Children age 8 and older welcome
ANIMALS:	Not allowed; Resident dog
HANDICAPPED:	Not handicapped accessible
DIETARY NEEDS:	Will accommodate guests' special dietary needs

Grand Marnier French Toast with Orange Rum Sauce

Makes 4 Servings

6   eggs
⅔   cup orange juice
⅓   cup Grand Marnier
⅓   cup milk
3   tablespoons sugar
¼   teaspoon vanilla extract
¼   teaspoon salt
1   tablespoon grated orange zest
8   (¾-inch-thick) slices French bread
3-4 tablespoons butter plus extra for serving
Powdered sugar

Orange rum sauce:
1   cup sugar
⅔   cup freshly squeezed orange juice
2   tablespoons dark rum
1   tablespoon curaçao (orange liqueur)
Coarsely grated zest of 1 orange

Beat eggs. Add orange juice, Grand Marnier, milk, sugar, vanilla, salt and orange zest; mix well. Dip bread into egg mixture, turning to coat. Put bread in a single layer in a baking dish. Pour remaining egg mixture over bread. Cover and refrigerate overnight, turning occasionally.

The next day, melt butter in large skillet over medium-high heat. Cook French toast until browned on each side. Cut French toast diagonally and arrange on a platter. Sprinkle with powdered sugar. Serve with butter and warm orange rum sauce.

For the orange rum sauce: In a small saucepan over low heat, bring sugar and orange juice to a boil, stirring constantly, then remove from heat. Stir in rum, curaçao and orange zest. Cool completely. Strain sauce and serve warm (if not using immediately, cover and refrigerate, then reheat).

A Boxwood Inn of Williamsburg

Designed to capture your heart, A Boxwood Inn of Williamsburg is located in an extensively renovated 1928 home. The inn is the perfect tranquil getaway, featuring luxurious beds, whirlpool tubs, antiques, cozy fireplace, spacious sun room and Williamsburg's "nicest back porch."

Located in the Architectural Preservation District, the inn is within walking distance of Colonial Williamsburg and just two blocks from the College of William & Mary. Garden lovers will marvel at the inn's beautiful, award-winning perennial gardens.

INNKEEPERS:	Steve & Sandi Zareski
ADDRESS:	708 Richmond Road
	Williamsburg, Virginia 23185
TELEPHONE:	(757) 221-6607; (888) 798-4333
E-MAIL:	host@boxwoodinn.com
WEBSITE:	www.boxwoodinn.com
ROOMS:	4 Rooms; Private baths
CHILDREN:	Children age 12 and older welcome
ANIMALS:	Not allowed; Resident dog
HANDICAPPED:	Not handicapped accessible
DIETARY NEEDS:	Will accommodate guests' special dietary needs

Praline-Topped Oven French Toast

Makes 8 to 10 Servings

Plan ahead, this French toast needs to be started the night before.

1   (12-ounce) loaf French bread, sliced into 1-inch-thick slices
8   large eggs
1½ cups milk
1½ cups half & half
2   teaspoons vanilla extract
½   teaspoon nutmeg
½   teaspoon cinnamon
Powdered sugar, for garnish

Praline topping:
1½ sticks butter, softened
1   tablespoon dark corn syrup
1½ cups packed brown sugar
1   cup chopped pecans

Butter a deep 10x15-inch baking pan. Fill pan with bread, laying slices flat and cutting to fit as needed. Beat eggs, milk, half & half, vanilla, nutmeg and cinnamon; pour over bread. Cover and refrigerate overnight.

The next morning, preheat oven to 350°F. Spread praline topping over ingredients in baking pan. Bake for 50 minutes. Let stand for 5 minutes. Sprinkle with powdered sugar, slice and serve.

For the praline topping: Melt butter in a small saucepan over medium heat. Add corn syrup and brown sugar; stir until mixture is smooth. Stir in pecans.

Applewood Colonial

The Applewood Colonial Bed & Breakfast is a stately, circa 1929 Georgian home built by the construction manager for the Colonial Williamsburg restoration. The same craftsmen who meticulously restored and reconstructed the 18th-century town, also used their skills to build Applewood in the classic Colonial style.

The hand-crafted architectural details found in the inn – such as Flemish-bond brick, seven-piece crown molding and brass mortise locks – are also found throughout the Colonial Williamsburg exhibition buildings.

INNKEEPERS:	Marty Jones
ADDRESS:	605 Richmond Road
	Williamsburg, Virginia 23185
TELEPHONE:	(757) 229-0205; (800) 899-2753
E-MAIL:	info@williamsburgbandb.com
WEBSITE:	www.williamsburgbandb.com
ROOMS:	2 Rooms; 2 Suites; Private baths
CHILDREN:	Call ahead
ANIMALS:	Not allowed
HANDICAPPED:	Not handicapped accessible
DIETARY NEEDS:	Will accommodate guests' special dietary needs

Peach French Toast

Makes 8 Servings

"Peaches make this upside-down French toast casserole so good, with just the right texture. Plan ahead, this French toast needs to be started the night before." ~ Innkeeper, Applewood Colonial Bed & Breakfast

1	stick butter
1	cup packed brown sugar
¼	cup sour cream
2	cups sliced, peeled fresh or frozen (thawed) peaches or canned, drained peaches
Nutmeg, to taste	
12	slices Pepperidge Farm sweet buttermilk bread, torn or cut into 1-inch pieces
6	large eggs
1½	cups milk or half & half
1	teaspoon vanilla extract
¼	cup chopped pecans, toasted
Powdered sugar, for garnish	

Melt butter in a small saucepan over low heat. Add brown sugar and stir until combined. Add sour cream and whisk until smooth; set aside to cool.

Spray a 9x13-inch casserole dish with non-stick cooking spray. Spread butter mixture over bottom of baking dish. Top with peaches. Sprinkle with nutmeg. Pile bread on top of peaches up to edge of casserole. Beat eggs, milk and vanilla; pour over bread. Cover and refrigerate overnight.

The next day, preheat oven to 375°F. Top French toast with pecans and bake for 1 hour. Cool slightly, then cut into squares, dust with powdered sugar and serve.

The Bell House

A lexander Graham Bell, the inventor of the telephone, called the Bell House home during summer months. This extraordinary, circa 1883 Victorian was built by Colonel J.O.P. Burnside, son of Civil War General Ambrose Burnside. Owned next by Alexander Graham Bell's father and then Alexander himself, the home overlooks a wide expanse of the Potomac River.

Step back in time and enjoy the historical ambiance of the house. Every detail reflects the quality and workmanship of a bygone era.

INNKEEPERS:	Phil & Anne Bolin
ADDRESS:	821 Irving Avenue
	Colonial Beach, Virginia 22443
TELEPHONE:	(804) 224-7000
E-MAIL:	thebolins@thebellhouse.com
WEBSITE:	www.thebellhouse.com
ROOMS:	4 Rooms; Private baths
CHILDREN:	Not allowed
ANIMALS:	Not allowed
HANDICAPPED:	Not handicapped accessible
DIETARY NEEDS:	Will accommodate guests' special dietary needs

Banana-Stuffed Griddle Bread

Makes 2 to 4 Servings

"I serve this stuffed bread with scrambled eggs and mild Italian sausage or bacon. The plates always come back to the kitchen empty! It is best prepared the morning of serving." ~ Innkeeper, The Bell House

4   large eggs
¼   cup half & half
1   teaspoon vanilla extract
Cinnamon, to taste
4   (1- to 1½-inch-thick) slices French or Italian bread
2   bananas, sliced plus extra banana slices, for serving
Powdered sugar, for garnish
Maple syrup, for serving

Mix eggs, half & half, vanilla and cinnamon in a large plate or a wide dish. Cut each slice of bread almost through, making a pocket. Layer banana slices in bread pockets and press to seal. Soak stuffed bread in egg mixture, turning to coat all sides.

Preheat a greased griddle to 375°F or a skillet over medium heat. Cook bread until browned on each side. Put 1-2 slices of griddle bread on each plate. Top with banana slices. Sprinkle with powdered sugar and serve with maple syrup.

The Inn at Court Square

The Inn at Court Square, located in the oldest building in historic downtown Charlottesville, extends fine Southern hospitality in a beautifully restored 1785 home. This luxury inn features well-appointed guestrooms with fine antique furnishings and decorative objects, that may be purchased during your visit. Guests have even bought the beds they slept in during their visit!

Equipped with fireplaces and private baths with whirlpool tubs, the inn offers all the comforts of home.

INNKEEPERS:	Candace DeLoach
ADDRESS:	410 East Jefferson Street
	Charlottesville, Virginia 22902
TELEPHONE:	(434) 295-2800; (866) 466-2877
E-MAIL:	innatcourtsquare@aol.com
WEBSITE:	www.innatcourtsquare.com
ROOMS:	7 Rooms; Private baths
CHILDREN:	Children age 12 and older welcome
ANIMALS:	Not allowed
HANDICAPPED:	Not handicapped accessible
DIETARY NEEDS:	Will accommodate guests' special dietary needs

Orange Croissant Bread Pudding with Clementine Syrup

Makes 10 to 12 Servings

1⅔ cups milk
1⅔ cups whipping cream
¾ cup sugar
3 large eggs, beaten
2 teaspoons grated clementine or orange
1 teaspoon vanilla extract
12 croissants, halved
½ cup chopped pecans, toasted
Sifted powdered sugar, for garnish

Clementine syrup:
2 cups sugar
¼ cup water
Juice of ½ lemon
4 clementines or oranges, peeled and sectioned (seeded, if needed)

Combine milk, cream and sugar in a saucepan over low heat. Stir to dissolve sugar, then remove from heat and cool. When cool, add eggs, orange zest and vanilla; mix well. Arrange croissant bottoms in a buttered 9x13-inch baking dish. Sprinkle ½ of pecans over croissants. Top with croissants tops, then sprinkle with remaining pecans. Pour egg mixture over croissants. Let stand for 30 minutes, pressing croissants into liquid once or twice.

Preheat oven to 350°F. Put baking dish in a baking pan. Add enough boiling water to pan to come halfway up sides of baking dish. Bake for 40 minutes, or until pudding is set and golden brown on top. Sprinkle with powdered sugar and top with clementine syrup. Serve with extra clementine syrup.

For the clementine syrup: Bring sugar, water and lemon juice to a boil in a non-reactive 2½-quart saucepan; cook to a deep amber. Carefully add clementines (caramel will bubble up as clementine juice is released). Cook until reduced to a syrup consistency. Strain through a sieve and cool.

Cape Charles House

Cape Charles House Bed & Breakfast on Virginia's Eastern Shore invites you step back in time and enjoy a slower pace. The concentration of historic homes has placed the seven square block town on the National Register of Historic Places.

Relax at the tranquil beach that fronts the town, walk the jetty pier, take a sunset sail, pedal through town on guest bikes, bike the back roads, hike the nature trails at the Eastern Shore Wildlife Refuge, enjoy bird watching at Kiptopeke State Park, sip afternoon tea and later enjoy wine and cheese.

INNKEEPERS:	Bruce & Carol Evans
ADDRESS:	645 Tazewell Avenue
	Cape Charles, Virginia 23310
TELEPHONE:	(757) 331-4920
E-MAIL:	stay@capecharleshouse.com
WEBSITE:	www.capecharleshouse.com
ROOMS:	5 Rooms; Private baths
CHILDREN:	Children age 12 and older welcome
ANIMALS:	Not allowed
HANDICAPPED:	Not handicapped accessible
DIETARY NEEDS:	Will accommodate guests' special dietary needs

Savory Asparagus Croissants

Makes 4 Servings

"So elegant and impressive! A great do-ahead that always gets raves. Serve for breakfast, brunch or lunch." ~ Innkeeper, Cape Charles House Bed & Breakfast

4   croissants, sliced in half lengthwise
1½   cups grated Swiss cheese, divided
16   asparagus spears, cooked
Garlic salt, to taste
Black pepper, to taste
Chopped fresh dill, to taste
4   large eggs
1¼   cups half & half
⅛   teaspoon cayenne pepper
2   teaspoons Grey Poupon Dijon mustard
1   teaspoon nutmeg
½   teaspoon salt
White and black sesame seeds

Spray a 9x13-inch baking dish with non-stick cooking spray. Put croissant bottoms in baking dish. Sprinkle with ¾ cup of Swiss cheese. Top each croissant with 4 asparagus spears. Sprinkle with garlic salt, pepper and a little dill. Sprinkle with remaining ¾ cup of Swiss cheese.

Combine eggs, half & half, cayenne, mustard, nutmeg and salt; beat well. Dip croissant tops in egg mixture and place on top of croissants in baking dish. Pour remaining egg mixture over croissants. Top each croissant with a few white and black sesame seeds (at this point, the dish can be covered and refrigerated overnight).

Preheat oven to 375°F. Bake croissants for 15 minutes, or until egg mixture is set (if croissants are browning too quickly, loosely cover baking dish with foil). Carefully cut around croissants and lift onto warmed serving plates.

Serving suggestion: Put 3 strips of bacon and a cluster of grapes on a grape or ivy leaf on each plate and top with a pansy or marigold flower.

Apple Tree

A pple Tree Bed & Breakfast is located in Damascus, in the heart of the Virginia Highlands. Damascus is close to Mount Rogers, the highest mountain in Virginia. The inn is located on the Appalachian Trail and is a block from the Virginia Creeper Trail, a 34-mile biking, walking and horseback riding trail. Nearby streams offer some of the best trout fishing anywhere.

Apple Tree is a 95-year-old home in the kind of small town where strangers still smile and wave.

INNKEEPERS:	John & Beth Reese
ADDRESS:	115 East Laurel Avenue
	Damascus, Virginia 24236
TELEPHONE:	(877) 362-7753
E-MAIL:	appletree@naxs.com
WEBSITE:	www.appletreebnb.com
ROOMS:	3 Rooms; 2 Suites; Private baths
CHILDREN:	Welcome
ANIMALS:	Not allowed; Resident cats
HANDICAPPED:	Suites are handicapped accessible
DIETARY NEEDS:	Will accommodate guests' special dietary needs

Biscuit Bread Pudding

Makes 4 to 6 Servings

"A great way to use up leftover biscuits. The bread pudding also freezes well." ~ Innkeeper, Apple Tree Bed & Breakfast

8-12 biscuits, crumbled (see recipe on page 27)
1 stick butter or light margarine, melted
3 large egg yolks
9 large egg whites
1½ cups sugar
4 cups milk
1 teaspoon cinnamon
½ teaspoon nutmeg
1 cup raisins
2 tablespoons vanilla extract

Preheat oven to 350°F. Grease 3 mini-loaf pans. Put crumbled biscuits in a large bowl. Pour butter over biscuits. In a medium bowl, beat egg yolks, egg whites and sugar. Mix in milk, cinnamon and nutmeg; pour over biscuits and let stand until biscuits absorb some of the liquid. Stir in raisins and vanilla. Divide biscuit mixture among loaf pans. Bake for 1 hour, or until set. Cool, then remove from pans. Slice into squares and serve.

By the Side of the Road

B y the Side of the Road is a bed & breakfast built in a 1790, shortly after the American Revolution, by Mennonite settlers of the Shenandoah Valley. Experience the richness of the historical past and the luxurious amenities of the present, including whirlpools, featherbeds, golf packages, gourmet breakfasts and the finest lodging in the Shenandoah region.

"Let me live in my house by the side of the road and be a friend to man," states Sam Walter Foss' famous poem that aptly describes the hospitality you'll experience when you visit By the Side of the Road.

INNKEEPERS:	Janice & Dennis Fitzgerald
ADDRESS:	491 Garbers Church Road
	Harrisonburg, Virginia 22801
TELEPHONE:	(540) 801-0430
E-MAIL:	stay@bythesideoftheroad.com
WEBSITE:	www.bythesideoftheroad.com
ROOMS:	4 Suites; 1 Cottage; Private baths
CHILDREN:	Welcome
ANIMALS:	Not allowed; Resident dog
HANDICAPPED:	Not handicapped accessible
DIETARY NEEDS:	Will accommodate guests' special dietary needs

Apple Crêpes with Cranberry Sauce

Makes 6 Servings

12 crêpes (see crêpe recipe on page 105)
6 tart apples, peeled, cored and sliced ¼-inch thick
¼ cup sugar (up to ½ cup, depending on tartness of apples)
2 tablespoons cornstarch
¼ teaspoon nutmeg
½ teaspoon cinnamon
¼ teaspoon allspice
2 tablespoons lemon juice
1 teaspoon grated lemon zest
¾ stick unsalted butter

Cranberry sauce:
1 cup sugar
3 tablespoons cornstarch
2 cups cold water
2 cups fresh or frozen cranberries

Prepare crêpes according to recipe directions and stack between layers of waxed paper until ready to use. Put apples in a large bowl. In a small bowl, combine sugar, cornstarch, nutmeg, cinnamon, allspice, lemon juice and zest; sprinkle over apples and toss to coat well.

Melt butter in a skillet over medium heat. Add apples and cook until juices emerge. Lower heat, cover and simmer until apples are crisp-tender, about 5 minutes. Remove from heat and cover. Fill each crêpe with 2-3 spoonsful of warm apple filling. Fold crêpe sides to center. Top with hot cranberry sauce and serve.

For the cranberry sauce: Combine sugar and cornstarch. Put sugar mixture and cold water in a large saucepan over medium heat. Cook, stirring, until sugar begins to dissolve. Add cranberries and bring to a boil, stirring constantly. Lower heat and simmer until cranberries begin to burst and mixture thickens, about 5-7 minutes. Serve hot.

The Patriot Inn

The Patriot Inn is a circa 1784 architectural gem, located in the Olde Towne Portsmouth historical district. The busy Elizabeth River waterfront is reflected in the inn's hand-blown window panes, just as it has been for over 200 years. Shopping and antiquing on High Street are just steps away, as are the Portsmouth Naval Hospital and Tidewater Yacht Marina.

Bed chambers are attractively decorated and furnished with lots of historic charm, period-style antiques and reproductions. All beds feature goose down comforters and pillows.

INNKEEPERS:	Ronald D. & E. Verle Weiss
ADDRESS:	201 North Street
	Olde Towne Portsmouth, Virginia 23704
TELEPHONE:	(757) 391-0157
E-MAIL:	weisspatriot@aol.com
WEBSITE:	www.bbonline.com/va/patriot
ROOMS:	4 Rooms; Private baths
CHILDREN:	Children age 12 and older welcome
ANIMALS:	Not allowed
HANDICAPPED:	Not handicapped accessible
DIETARY NEEDS:	Will accommodate guests' special dietary needs

Cherry & Strawberry Crêpes

Makes 6 Servings

"These are a favorite of our guests. They often request them on return visits."
~ Innkeeper, The Patriot Inn Bed & Breakfast

Crêpes:
1   cup all-purpose flour
¼   teaspoon baking powder
¼   teaspoon salt
1   teaspoon sugar
4   large eggs
5⅓   tablespoons butter, melted
2   cups milk

Filling:
1   (20-ounce) can cherry pie filling (or other favorite flavor)
1   (10-ounce) package frozen sliced sweetened strawberries
Whipped cream, for serving

For the crêpes: In a medium bowl, combine flour, baking powder, salt and sugar. In a large bowl, beat eggs. Add flour mixture to eggs and mix well. Stir in butter, then stir in milk. If time allows, let batter stand for 30 minutes (this yields more tender crêpes).

Pour ¼ cup of batter into a crêpe pan or a skillet over medium heat. With a quick wrist action, swirl batter to cover bottom of pan. Cook until light brown on the first side, turn and cook the other side for just a few seconds.

For the filling: Fill each crêpe with pie filling and strawberries (reserve some pie filling and strawberries for topping crêpes). Fold up crêpes. Put 3 crêpes on each of 6 plates. Top with whipped cream, a little pie filling and a few strawberries to serve.

The Virginia Cliffe Inn

The Virginia Cliffe Inn is nestled among the trees in the settlement of Glen Allen, 12 miles north of Richmond. The six-acre grounds front the historic Mountain Road – the path Thomas Jefferson traveled on his trips from Charlottesville to Richmond and Williamsburg.

In winter, sip spiced tea in front of the fireplace in the wood-paneled den. In summer, sit in the backyard overlooking the rose garden and enjoy a cool drink.

INNKEEPERS:	James & Margaret Clifton
ADDRESS:	2900 Mountain Road
	Glen Allen, Virginia 23060
TELEPHONE:	(877) 254-3346
E-MAIL:	vacliffe@aol.com
WEBSITE:	www.vacliffeinn.com
ROOMS:	3 Rooms; 1 Suite; 1 Cottage; Private baths
CHILDREN:	Call ahead
ANIMALS:	Call ahead; Resident swans
HANDICAPPED:	Not handicapped accessible
DIETARY NEEDS:	Will accommodate guests' special dietary needs

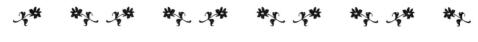

Cheese Blintz Casserole

Makes 6 to 8 Servings

"This is our most requested recipe." ~ Innkeeper, The Virginia Cliffe Inn

Cheese filling:
1   (8-ounce) package cream cheese, softened
2   (15-ounce) containers ricotta cheese
¼   cup lemon juice (about 1 lemon)
2   large eggs
¼   cup sugar
Pinch of salt

Blintzes:
2   sticks butter or margarine, melted
2   large eggs
½   cup sugar
1   cup all-purpose flour
1   tablespoon baking powder
Pinch of salt
¼   cup milk
1   teaspoon vanilla extract
Strawberry jam or jelly, for serving
Sliced fresh strawberries, for garnish

For the cheese filling: Mix cheese filling ingredients with a mixer or in a food processor until smooth.

For the blintzes: Combine butter, eggs, sugar, flour, baking powder, salt, milk and vanilla; stir until smooth. Spread half of batter in a greased 9x13-inch baking dish. Pour cheese filling over batter and spread gently and evenly with a rubber spatula (do not mix filling with batter). If time allows, cover and chill well.

Spread remaining batter over filling (at this point, you can cover the casserole and refrigerate or freeze). Preheat oven to 300°F. Bake for 90 minutes. Cool slightly. Warm jam or jelly and spread over blintzes as a glaze. Slice and serve topped with sliced strawberries.

Egg Dishes & Breakfast Entrées

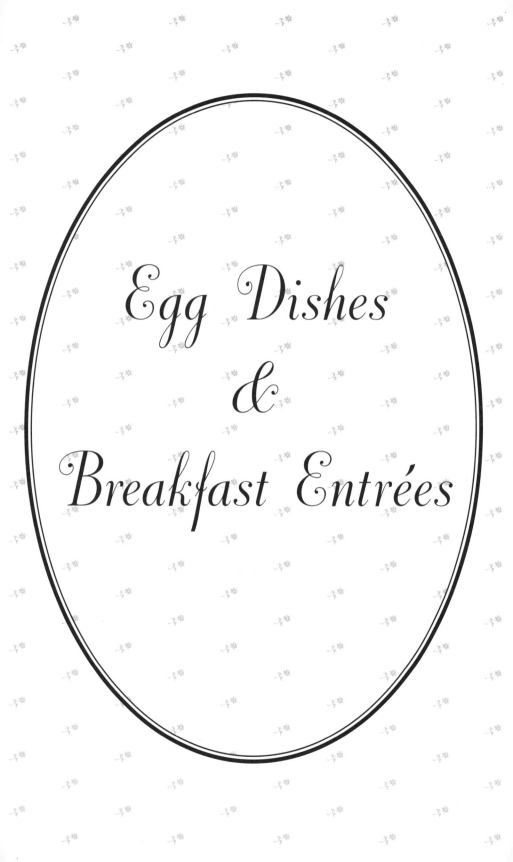

Egg Dishes
&
Breakfast Entrées

The William Miller House

The William Miller House is located in the Fan District, which is listed on the National Register of Historic Places, and is just minutes from downtown Richmond. The Fan is also home to Richmond's famous Monument Avenue, long recognized as one of 12 grand American avenues and one of the finest examples of urban and architectural design in the 19th- and early 20th-centuries.

A typical breakfast might include fresh vegetable and herb frittata or *rösti* potatoes with poached eggs and spoonbread with maple butter.

INNKEEPERS: Patricia Daniels & Mike Rohde
ADDRESS: 1129 Floyd Avenue
Richmond, Virginia 23220
TELEPHONE: (804) 254-2928
E-MAIL: innkeeper@ourfanhomes.com
WEBSITE: www.ourfanhomes.com
ROOMS: 2 Rooms; Private baths
CHILDREN: Not allowed
ANIMALS: Not allowed; Resident dogs
HANDICAPPED: Not handicapped accessible
DIETARY NEEDS: Call ahead

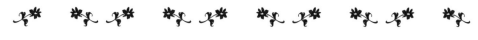

Miller House Poached Eggs with Boursin Sauce

Makes 4 Servings

"This recipe can be used for breakfast, brunch or a light supper." ~ Innkeeper, The William Miller House

20-28 asparagus spears, trimmed and scraped with a vegetable peeler
2   tablespoons unsalted butter, divided
1   tablespoon all-purpose flour
5   tablespoons Boursin cheese (packaged or homemade)*
¾   cup whole milk or half & half
8   extra-large eggs
1   tablespoon chopped parsley or other seasonal herbs, for garnish

Steam asparagus for 3-5 minutes (depending on thickness), just until tender. Transfer asparagus to an ice water bath to stop cooking and preserve its bright green color; set aside to drain on paper towels.

Melt 1 tablespoon of butter in a small saucepan over medium-low heat. Add flour and cook, stirring, for 1-2 minutes. Whisk in Boursin cheese and milk or half & half; cook until thickened and smooth (if sauce gets too thick, thin it with a little more milk). Poach eggs to desired doneness. Melt remaining 1 tablespoon of butter in a separate skillet over low heat. Add asparagus and cook just to warm it.

To assemble: Place 5-7 asparagus spears in a single layer on each plate. Top with 2 poached eggs and cheese sauce. Sprinkle with chopped parsley or other seasonal herbs to garnish.

~*Note: Boursin cheese is a soft, spreadable, creamy white cheese often flavored with herbs, sun-dried tomatoes, etc. It is available in the cheese section of most groceries.

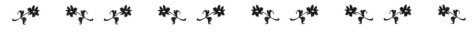

Thornrose House at Gypsy Hill

C ome enjoy the atmosphere of a slower-paced era at the Georgian Revival-style Thornrose House at Gypsy Hill. Located in Staunton, the inn offers spacious greenery with its acre of gardens and the 300-acre Gypsy Hill Park across the street. The downtown historic districts, unique shops, fine restaurants and Shenandoah Shakespeare Blackfriars Playhouse are within walking distance or a short, free trolley ride.

Amenities include comfortable robes and an assortment of fine soaps and shampoos. Chocolates and fresh flowers provide the finishing touches.

INNKEEPERS:	Otis & Suzy Huston
ADDRESS:	531 Thornrose Avenue
	Staunton, Virginia 24401
TELEPHONE:	(540) 885-7026; (800) 861-4338
E-MAIL:	innkeeper@thornrosehouse.com
WEBSITE:	www.thornrosehouse.com
ROOMS:	5 Rooms; Private baths
CHILDREN:	Children age 5 and older welcome
ANIMALS:	Not allowed; Resident cats
HANDICAPPED:	Not handicapped accessible
DIETARY NEEDS:	Will accommodate guests' special dietary needs

Eggs Florentine

Makes 2 to 4 Servings

"This recipe is adapted from a 1983 Cooking Light *cookbook recipe. I have made several changes, giving it our personal stamp and making it a little more heart-healthy." ~ Innkeeper, Thornrose House at Gypsy Hill*

1 · pound fresh spinach
4   large eggs, poached
2   whole-wheat English muffins, split
1   tablespoon butter, melted
4   thin slices turkey ham
4   slices tomato

Tarragon hollandaise sauce:
⅓   cup low-fat mayonnaise
2   tablespoons water
2   teaspoons fresh lemon juice
1   teaspoon chopped fresh tarragon leaves
Dash of black pepper

Bring a little water to a simmer in a deep skillet. Add spinach, cover and steam until nicely wilted; drain and keep warm. Toast English muffins and brush lightly with butter. Put a slice of ham and a slice of tomato on each muffin half. Top with spinach, 1 poached egg and some hollandaise sauce. Serve 1-2 muffin halves per guest.

For the hollandaise sauce: Combine hollandaise sauce ingredients in a saucepan over medium-low heat and cook until warmed through.

Stonewall Jackson Inn

The Stonewall Jackson Inn is a restored, circa 1885 mansion unique to the Shenandoah Valley. Two Boston architects adapted the traditional Queen Anne to a stone-and-shingled New England cottage style. Thus, the inn looks and feels like an old summer home in Newport or Bar Harbor.

The inn uses the finest Virginia staples in its recipes, such as Smithfield ham and local sausages and apples. These are featured in gourmet breakfast presentations such as cheese and smoked salmon omelets and croissant French toast stuffed with fresh strawberries.

INNKEEPERS:	Wayne Engel & Roger Engel
ADDRESS:	547 East Market Street
	Harrisonburg, Virginia 22801
TELEPHONE:	(540) 433-8233; (800) 445-5330
E-MAIL:	info@stonewalljacksoninn.com
WEBSITE:	www.stonewalljacksoninn.com
ROOMS:	10 Rooms; Private baths
CHILDREN:	Children age 12 and older welcome
ANIMALS:	Not allowed
HANDICAPPED:	Not handicapped accessible
DIETARY NEEDS:	Will accommodate guests' special dietary needs

Eggs Orleans

Makes 4 Servings

"Eggs Orleans is poached eggs over crab cakes and tomatoes on English muffins, blanketed with hollandaise sauce. Serve with fresh fruit, roasted potatoes and sautéed apples." ~ Innkeeper, Stonewall Jackson Inn Bed & Breakfast

Crab cakes:
16   ounces quality lump crabmeat
1   large egg
3   tablespoons mayonnaise
2   teaspoons Dijon mustard
1   teaspoon Worcestershire sauce
Splash of liquid crab boil
1   teaspoon Louisiana hot sauce
1   tablespoon grated carrot
1   tablespoon diced roasted red pepper
1   tablespoon sliced green onions
Bread crumbs
2   tablespoons vegetable oil or butter

Eggs:
1½   teaspoons white vinegar
8   large eggs
4   English muffins, split and toasted
½   cup hollandaise sauce (see recipes on page 113 and 117)
8   slices tomato

For the crab cakes: Combine all crab cake ingredients, except oil or butter, using enough bread crumbs to help form cakes. Make 8 relatively thin cakes the size of an English muffin. Heat oil or butter in a skillet over medium heat. Cook crab cakes until golden brown; drain on paper towels.

For the eggs: Bring 4 cups of water and white vinegar to a boil (the vinegar helps the eggs coagulate). Gently crack eggs into water. Cook for about 3 minutes, until eggs are set and yolks are still soft. Remove eggs with a slotted spoon, rocking the spoon over a towel to drain excess water.

Put 2 English muffin halves on each plate. Top each with a slice of tomato and a crab cake. Gently top with 1 poached egg. Spoon 1 tablespoon of hollandaise over each egg. Sprinkle with paprika to serve.

Bay View Waterfront

B ay View Waterfront Bed & Breakfast is located on a hill overlooking
Occohannock Creek with an expansive view to the Chesapeake Bay
and a dock to deep water. Guests of this large, gracious home can enjoy
reading, fishing, crabbing, biking, swimming in the pool or the creek, a
small beach, croquet, basketball, volleyball, a full country breakfast and
140 acres of woods, farmland and creek shore to hike and explore.

Bedrooms are meant to make guests feel comfortable. They have antiques,
local artwork, wonderful views, books and the Eastern Shore guidebook.

INNKEEPERS:	Wayne & Mary Will Browning
ADDRESS:	35350 Copes Drive
	Belle Haven, Virginia 23306
TELEPHONE:	(757) 442-6963; (800) 442-6966
E-MAIL:	browning@esva.net
WEBSITE:	www.bbhost.com/bvwaterfront
ROOMS:	1 Room; 1 Suite; Private baths
CHILDREN:	Welcome
ANIMALS:	Not allowed; Resident dogs
HANDICAPPED:	Not handicapped accessible
DIETARY NEEDS:	Will accommodate guests' special dietary needs

Bay View Eggs Benedict

Makes 1 to 2 Servings

"An Eastern Shore twist to a breakfast favorite." ~ Innkeeper, Bay View Waterfront Bed & Breakfast

1   English muffin, split
½   cup cooked fresh crabmeat
2   slices country ham
2   large eggs, poached

Hollandaise sauce:
3   large egg yolks
2   teaspoons lemon juice
¼   teaspoon salt
White pepper, to taste
½   teaspoon Dijon mustard (optional)
1   stick butter, melted and kept warm

Gently warm or toast English muffin halves. Top with crabmeat, ham and poached eggs. Top with hollandaise sauce and serve.

For the hollandaise sauce: Blend egg yolks, lemon juice, salt, white pepper and mustard in a blender on low speed for about 30 seconds. With blender running on low speed, slowly drizzle in melted butter until blades are coated, then blend on high speed for a few seconds. Serve immediately.

The Richard Johnston Inn

G uests of the Richard Johnston Inn can experience the charm of the candle-lit courtyard, stroll to wonderful restaurants, shop to their heart's content in numerous antique and gift shops or just relax. In the morning, wake to fresh baked goods served in the large Federal-style dining room at a table set with fine china, silver, crystal and linens.

The Kitchen House Room is a very quiet, private room that served as the original kitchen in the 1700s. Located off the courtyard, the room has a brick floor and a large fireplace with the original pots, pans and grid irons.

INNKEEPERS:	Bonnie L. DeLelys
ADDRESS:	711 Caroline Street
	Fredericksburg, Virginia 22401
TELEPHONE:	(540) 899-7606; (877) 557-0770
E-MAIL:	rjohnstoninn@staffnet.com
WEBSITE:	www.bbonline.com/va/richardjohnston
ROOMS:	9 Rooms; 2 Suites; Private baths
CHILDREN:	Welcome in 2 rooms
ANIMALS:	Welcome in 2 rooms; Resident dog
HANDICAPPED:	Not handicapped accessible
DIETARY NEEDS:	Will accommodate guests' special dietary needs

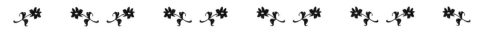

Ham Cups with Mornay Sauce

Makes 6 to 12 Servings

1 tablespoon butter
1 clove garlic, minced
2 cups sliced mushrooms
2 tablespoons chopped parsley
1 (10-ounce) package frozen spinach, thawed and drained
12 round slices ham
8 ounces feta cheese, crumbled
18 large eggs
1½ cups half & half
Fresh tomato slices, for garnish

Mornay sauce:
½ stick unsalted butter
¼ cup all-purpose flour
2½ cups milk, warmed
¼ cup grated Parmesan cheese
¼ cup grated Swiss or Gruyère cheese
Pinch each of nutmeg and cayenne pepper
Salt and white pepper, to taste

Preheat oven to 200°F. Melt butter in a skillet over medium heat. Add garlic and cook just until it starts to brown. Add mushrooms and parsley; cook until mushrooms are soft. Add spinach and cook until heated through.

Cut a slit halfway through each ham slice and fold to make a cup. Put ham "cup" in a muffin cup. Add ¼ cup of spinach mixture to each ham cup. Top with 1 tablespoon of feta cheese. Bake for 1 hour. Beat eggs and half & half. Soft scramble the eggs. Fill ham cups with eggs. Top with Mornay sauce. Serve 1-2 ham cups per person, garnished with tomato slices.

For the Mornay sauce: Melt butter in a saucepan over medium-low heat. Add flour and cook, stirring, for 3 minutes. Whisk in milk. Bring to a simmer, lower heat to low and cook, stirring often, for 8-10 minutes, until thickened. Stir in cheese until melted. Add nutmeg and cayenne. Season with salt and white pepper.

Old Massanutten Lodge

The Old Massanutten Lodge is set on six acres at the end of a quiet country road in the heart of the Shenandoah Valley at the western base of Massanutten Peak. Here you can relax and enjoy the beauty of nature, wander the garden or go horseback riding at a stable right next door.

Built and operated for its first 50 years as a day resort, this 1920s-era stone and stucco lodge has been carefully restored yet fully modernized. In its heyday, the lodge hosted cavern tours, swimming, dancing and parties, and provided memories for many guests from both near and far.

INNKEEPERS:	Margie & Guy Vlasits
ADDRESS:	3448 Caverns Drive
	Keezletown, Virginia 22832
TELEPHONE:	(540) 269-8800
E-MAIL:	m-gvlasits@juno.com
WEBSITE:	www.oldmassanuttenlodge.com
ROOMS:	2 Rooms; 1 Suite; Private baths
CHILDREN:	Welcome
ANIMALS:	Not allowed; Resident cats
HANDICAPPED:	Handicapped accessible
DIETARY NEEDS:	Will accommodate guests' special dietary needs

Creamy Veggies with Spinach, Sausage & Eggs

Makes 6 Servings

1   pound link sausage (18 small sausages)
3   cloves garlic, minced
6   carrots, thinly sliced
4   green onions, white and green parts thinly sliced
1½ cups half & half
½   cup grated Parmesan cheese
6   cups fresh or 1 (10-ounce) package frozen spinach, steamed and squeezed dry
6   hard-boiled eggs, sliced
Paprika, for garnish

Cook sausage in a skillet over medium heat until done. Remove sausage and keep warm; reserve any grease in skillet. Add garlic, carrots and white parts of green onions to skillet. Stir in half & half and Parmesan cheese (add more half & half, if needed, so mixture is not runny, but not thick). Add green parts of green onions and cook for 2 minutes.

Divide spinach among plates. Spoon creamed vegetables and sauce over spinach. Top with 1 sliced hard-boiled egg. Sprinkle with paprika. Serve with 3 sausages on the side and with fried apples and whole-wheat biscuits or bran muffins with butter and jam or honey.

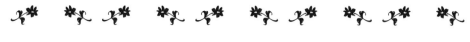

Highland Farm & Inn

The Highland Farm & Inn is a small bed & breakfast set in the midst of Virginia's hunt and wine country, overlooking the Rappahannock River with views of the Blue Ridge Mountains. The accommodations, tastefully furnished with family antiques, offer a secluded, quiet and romantic point from which to explore the area.

Highland Farm is located on 36 acres and is actively engaged in the raising of Thoroughbred horses and cattle, bringing an added dimension to your "get away" experience.

INNKEEPERS:	Ralph & Linda Robinson
ADDRESS:	10981 Lee's Mill Road
	Remington, Virginia 22734
TELEPHONE:	(540) 439-0088
E-MAIL:	innkeeper@highlandfarminn.com
WEBSITE:	www.highlandfarminn.com
ROOMS:	2 Rooms; 1 Cottage; Private baths
CHILDREN:	Children age 12 and older welcome
ANIMALS:	Not allowed; Resident dog & horses
HANDICAPPED:	Handicapped accessible
DIETARY NEEDS:	Will accommodate guests' special dietary needs

Highland Eggs

Makes 2 Servings

"This egg dish uses fresh produce from the garden. Cooked bacon can be added. Sometimes I use lightly cooked asparagus in place of the tomatoes." - Innkeeper, Highland Farm & Inn

White sauce:
2   tablespoons butter
2   tablespoons all-purpose flour
1   cup milk
Salt and white or black pepper, to taste
Dijon mustard, to taste

Eggs:
Italian salad dressing
4   slices peeled tomato
2   English muffins, split
4   large eggs
1   tablespoon chopped fresh basil
1   cup grated cheddar cheese

For the white sauce: Melt butter in a saucepan over medium-low heat. Stir in flour and cook, stirring, for 3 minutes. Whisk in milk. Bring to a simmer, lower heat to low and cook, stirring often, for 8-10 minutes, until thickened. Add salt, pepper and mustard to taste.

For the eggs: Preheat broiler. Sprinkle Italian dressing over tomatoes. Top with basil. Toast English muffins. Poach eggs. Drain tomatoes and put 1 tomato slice on each of muffin half. Top with 1 poached egg, ¼ cup of white sauce and ¼ cup of cheese. Broil until cheese is melted and bubbly.

Airville Plantation

Through ivy-covered gates, at the end of a lane bordered by tall cedar and dogwood trees, stands Airville Plantation Bed & Breakfast, near Williamsburg. Slip back in time as you sit on the veranda and watch the sunset over 400 acres of gardens, meadows and woodlands.

In the library, read or reflect before a blazing fire. The parlor beckons for afternoon tea accompanied by a fresh baked sweet. In summer, relax by the pool or take a long walk down a wooded trail.

INNKEEPERS:	Kathie & Larry Cohen
ADDRESS:	6423 T.C. Walker Road
	Gloucester, Virginia 23061
TELEPHONE:	(804) 694-0287
E-MAIL:	airville@visi.net
WEBSITE:	www.airvilleplantation.com
ROOMS:	2 Rooms; 1 Cottage; Private & shared baths
CHILDREN:	Children age 12 and older welcome
ANIMALS:	Not allowed; Resident dogs & cats
HANDICAPPED:	Not handicapped accessible
DIETARY NEEDS:	Will accommodate guests' special dietary needs

Baked Egg in Tomato

Makes 4 Servings

"This recipe came from Pete Holladay, former owner of the Holladay House Bed & Breakfast in Orange, Virginia. We always have more tomatoes in our garden than we know what to do with and he took pity and shared!" ~ Innkeeper, Airville Plantation Bed & Breakfast

4   large ripe tomatoes
¼   cup grated sharp cheddar cheese
¼   cup fresh soft bread crumbs
1   tablespoon chopped parsley
¼   teaspoon salt
⅛   teaspoon black pepper
4   large eggs
2   tablespoons butter, melted
Chopped fresh basil, for garnish

Preheat oven to 425°F. Cut off tops of tomatoes and scoop out pulp. Put tomatoes in a greased 8x8-inch baking pan and bake for 5-7 minutes. Mix cheese, bread crumbs, parsley, salt and pepper. Break 1 egg into each tomato. Add about 2 tablespoons of cheese mixture to each tomato, then drizzle with melted butter. Bake for about 20 minutes, until eggs are set. Garnish with fresh basil to serve.

Briar Patch

BED & BREAKFAST

Nestled in the foothills of the Blue Ridge and Shenandoah Mountains, the Briar Patch Bed & Breakfast offers charm and hospitality to match its historic location. Briar Patch is a historic circa 1905 farm on 47 rolling acres in the heart of Virginia horse, antique and wine country, just 20 minutes from Dulles Airport and 45 minutes from Washington, D.C.

The Sunflower Room is bright and sunny with a brass, queen-size bed, antique furnishings and great mountain views.

INNKEEPERS:	Ellen Goldberg & Dan Haendel
ADDRESS:	23130 Briar Patch Lane
	Middleburg, Virginia 20117
TELEPHONE:	(703) 327-5911; (866) 327-5911
E-MAIL:	info@briarpatchbandb.com
WEBSITE:	www.briarpatchbandb.com
ROOMS:	8 Rooms; 1 Cottage; Private & shared baths
CHILDREN:	Welcome; Call ahead
ANIMALS:	Call ahead
HANDICAPPED:	Call ahead
DIETARY NEEDS:	Will accommodate guests' special dietary needs

Baked Eggs with Havarti & Dill

Makes 1 Serving

"Our most popular dish and the easiest to prepare. Simply multiply as needed for additional guests." - Innkeeper, Briar Patch Bed & Breakfast

1   teaspoon butter, melted
1   tablespoon cream
2   large eggs
Salt and black pepper, to taste
Grated Havarti cheese, to taste
Chopped fresh dill, to taste

Preheat oven to 425°F. Butter a 4-ounce ramekin or an individual baking dish with melted butter. Add cream. Carefully crack eggs into ramekin. Season with salt and pepper. Sprinkle with cheese and then dill. Bake for 8-10 minutes, or until egg white is firm and center is still soft.

Stonewall Jackson Inn

The Stonewall Jackson Inn is a restored, circa 1885 mansion that is unique to the Shenandoah Valley. Just who built the inn is obscure, but it is believed to have been a New England sea captain who moved to Harrisonburg after marrying a valley debutante.

The mansion was constructed to entertain on a grand scale. There are three floors with a large Queen Anne "living hallway" entrance and beamed ceilings. The stairways and doors were made wide to accommodate the hoop skirts, as guests would enter from their carriage to the front veranda.

INNKEEPERS:	Wayne Engel & Roger Engel
ADDRESS:	547 East Market Street
	Harrisonburg, Virginia 22801
TELEPHONE:	(540) 433-8233; (800) 445-5330
E-MAIL:	info@stonewalljacksoninn.com
WEBSITE:	www.stonewalljacksoninn.com
ROOMS:	10 Rooms; Private baths
CHILDREN:	Children age 12 and older welcome
ANIMALS:	Not allowed
HANDICAPPED:	Not handicapped accessible
DIETARY NEEDS:	Will accommodate guests' special dietary needs

Crab Soufflé

Makes 8 Servings

"We serve this soufflé with rosemary potatoes and locally made sausage. You can spice it up by substituting seasoned salt or Old Bay Seasoning for the salt in the recipe. Plan ahead, this dish needs to be started the night before." - Innkeeper, Stonewall Jackson Inn Bed & Breakfast

1	tablespoon butter
12	eggs
½	cup skim or whole milk
1	teaspoon salt, seasoned salt or Old Bay seasoning
½	teaspoon black pepper
½	teaspoon dried dill weed
1	cup chopped crabmeat
1	(8-ounce) package cream cheese, cut into cubes
2	green onions, chopped

Paprika, for topping

Rub butter over the bottom of an 8x8-inch baking dish to coat. Beat eggs, milk, salt, pepper and dill. Stir in crab, cream cheese and green onions. Pour egg mixture into baking dish, cover and refrigerate overnight.

The next day, preheat oven to 350°F. Sprinkle egg mixture with paprika. Bake for 45-50 minutes, or until center is set.

Oak Grove Plantation

Guests of the Oak Grove Plantation Bed & Breakfast can stay near the plantation house for wildflower walks, reading, biking, hiking on over 400 acres or a reiki session. Or, you can visit Civil War battlefields, the last capital of the Confederacy in Danville, shop for antiques, go to Buggs Island Lake or Hyco Lake for swimming and boating, play golf, take in a minor league baseball game and much more!

Guest rooms are large and include sitting areas. The Federalist Blue Room has a lacy canopy bed and a wood-burning fireplace.

INNKEEPERS:	Pickett Craddock
ADDRESS:	1245 Cluster Springs Road
	Cluster Springs, Virginia 24535
TELEPHONE:	(434) 575-7137; (877) 343-7871
E-MAIL:	info@oakgroveplantation.com
WEBSITE:	www.oakgroveplantation.com
ROOMS:	3 Rooms; 1 Suite; Private & shared baths
CHILDREN:	Welcome
ANIMALS:	Dogs welcome; Resident dog
HANDICAPPED:	Handicapped accessible
DIETARY NEEDS:	Will accommodate guests' special dietary needs

Cluster Springs Egg Puff

Makes 6 to 8 Servings

"This is great with homemade salsa. It can be made the night before, covered and refrigerated, then baked in the morning." ~ Innkeeper, Oak Grove Plantation Bed & Breakfast

10   large eggs
½   cup unbleached all-purpose flour
1   teaspoon baking powder
½   teaspoon salt
1   (16-ounce) carton low-fat small-curd cottage cheese
2   cups grated low-fat (part-skim) mozzarella
3   tablespoons canola oil
1   (4-ounce) can diced green chilies, drained
Paprika, for garnish

Preheat oven to 350°F. Spray a 9x13-inch baking pan with non-stick cooking spray. Beat eggs. Add remaining ingredients, except paprika, and mix well. Pour mixture into baking pan. Sprinkle with paprika and bake for 35-40 minutes.

Old Spring Farm

Old Spring Farm Bed & Breakfast offers lodging in the circa 1883 farmhouse or the Country Retreat House. Country French décor complements period pieces and collectibles in the rooms of the Farmhouse. Enjoy fine lithographs, museum prints and original paintings throughout. A walking tour of the farm affords exercise and the opportunity to cuddle Manx kittens and view the newest foals frolicking and lambs leaping.

Old Spring Farm was rated as "The best bed & breakfast in southwest Virginia" in 2002 by *City Magazine Roanoke*.

INNKEEPERS:	Suzanne V. Pabst
ADDRESS:	7629 Charity Highway
	Woolwine, Virginia 24185
TELEPHONE:	(276) 930-3404
E-MAIL:	Not available
WEBSITE:	www.oldspringfarm.com
ROOMS:	6 Rooms; Private & shared baths
CHILDREN:	Children age 6 and older welcome
ANIMALS:	Not allowed; Resident dog & cat
HANDICAPPED:	Call ahead
DIETARY NEEDS:	Will accommodate guests' special dietary needs

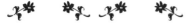 

Creamed Salmon with Poached Eggs on Waffles

Makes 4 Servings

"This recipe is elegant enough for breakfast, brunch or a light dinner. It can also be served over English muffins or any good toasted and buttered bread. It seems fussy, but believe me, once you've done it, you will be eager to do it again and again – guests love it!" ~ Innkeeper, Old Spring Farm Bed & Breakfast

1	tablespoon plus ½ stick butter
3	green onions, sliced
1	cup sliced mushrooms
¼	cup all-purpose flour
2	cups half & half

Salt and black pepper, to taste

1	teaspoon dried tarragon (or 1 tablespoon chopped fresh tarragon)
1	teaspoon chopped fresh dill plus extra for garnish
1	teaspoon chopped fresh parsley plus extra for garnish
1	cup green peas (if serving for lunch or dinner)
4	waffles (see recipes on pages 79 and 83)
1	(14-ounce) can Alaskan pink salmon, drained
4	large eggs, poached

Melt 1 tablespoon of butter in a skillet over medium heat. Add mushrooms and green onions; cook until softened, then set aside. Melt the ½ stick of butter in a saucepan over low heat. Stir in flour and cook for 3 minutes. Remove from heat and, stirring constantly, add half & half. Add green onion mixture, salt, pepper, tarragon, parsley and peas. Heat sauce, but do not let it boil (sauce may be held in a double boiler over water at a low simmer).

Put 1 waffle on each plate (if waffles are cold, warm them for 10 minutes in a preheated 200°F oven). Top waffles with salmon (salmon does not have to be heated). Top with a poached egg and some sauce. Garnish with fresh dill and/or parsley to serve.

1848 Island Manor House

Prior to the Civil War, two young gentlemen, Dr. Nathaniel Smith and Joseph Kenny pooled their resources and built a large T-shaped house. One day, a young lady named Sarah came to visit from Baltimore. Joseph fell in love and married her. Her sister, Juliet, came for the wedding. Cupid struck again and Nathaniel soon married her. However, the sisters found that, as much as they cared for each other, they did not enjoy living under the same roof. To save their friendship – and their marriages – the couple split the house. After 150 years, the two houses came together again as the 1848 Island Manor House, continuing the romance of a bygone era.

INNKEEPERS:	Jerry Prewitt & Andrew (A.D.) Dawson
ADDRESS:	4160 Main Street
	Chincoteague Island, Virginia 23336
TELEPHONE:	(757) 336-5436; (800) 852-1505
E-MAIL:	hosts@islandmanor.com
WEBSITE:	www.islandmanor.com
ROOMS:	8 Rooms; Private & shared baths
CHILDREN:	Children age 10 and older welcome
ANIMALS:	Not allowed
HANDICAPPED:	Not handicapped accessible
DIETARY NEEDS:	Will accommodate guests' special dietary needs

Cheesy Eggs

Makes 1 Serving

"A quick and easy recipe for individual servings." ~ Innkeeper, 1848 Island Manor House

2   slices Canadian bacon
Grated sharp cheddar cheese
2   eggs, beaten
1   tablespoon heavy whipping cream
Paprika, to taste
Grated Parmesan cheese

Preheat oven to 350°F. Spray a 10-ounce ramekin with non-stick cooking spray. Overlap slices of Canadian bacon in bottom of ramekin. Add enough cheddar cheese to make a nest. Break eggs into center of cheese nest. Drizzle whipping cream around cheese (be careful not to mix cream and eggs). Sprinkle paprika over all. Bake for 15 minutes, then remove from oven and sprinkle Parmesan cheese over all. Bake for 15 minutes more and serve.

Hearth n' Holly Inn

W hat says relaxation more then a wrap-around porch with plenty of comfortable seating and a porch swing? For the more energetic, the Shenandoah National Park has a multitude of circuit hikes and hikes to waterfalls. The park entrance is 20 minutes from the inn's front door.

Breakfast is served in the solar room with a wonderful mountain vista, and includes homemade muffins and breads, and delicious entrées such as elegant French toast, eggs celant or gingerbread pancakes with lemon sauce.

INNKEEPERS:	Dennis & Doris Brown
ADDRESS:	46 Songbird Lane
	Penn Laird, Virginia 22846
TELEPHONE:	(800) 209-1379
E-MAIL:	hhinn@shentel.net
WEBSITE:	www.hearthnholly.com
ROOMS:	3 Rooms; Private baths
CHILDREN:	Welcome
ANIMALS:	Not allowed; Resident dog & cat
HANDICAPPED:	Not handicapped accessible
DIETARY NEEDS:	Will accommodate guests' special dietary needs

Rolled Ham & Gruyère Omelet

Makes 6 Servings

You can substitute eight slices of crisply cooked, crumbled bacon or eight ounces of cut-up cooked link sausage for the ham in this delicious omelet.

½	cup all-purpose flour
1	cup milk
2	tablespoons butter or margarine, melted
½	teaspoon salt
4	large eggs
1	cup coarsely chopped ham
1	small onion, chopped
1½	cups grated Gruyère or Swiss cheese
1	cup chopped fresh spinach or thawed, well drained frozen chopped spinach plus whole fresh spinach leaves, for garnish

Preheat oven to 350°F. Line a 15x10-inch rimmed baking sheet with foil. Generously grease foil. Beat flour, milk, butter, salt and eggs until well blended; pour mixture into baking sheet. Sprinkle with ham and onion.

Bake for 15-18 minutes, until eggs are set. Immediately sprinkle with cheese and spinach. Roll up omelet, beginning at narrow end, using foil to lift and roll it. Cut omelet into 1½-inch slices and serve on plates garnished with fresh spinach leaves.

Grace Manor Inn

The Grace Manor Inn is conveniently located in the heart of the Fan district. Listed on the National and State Registers of Historic Places, the inn is only one block from Richmond's historic Monument District and is within walking distance of many restaurants and museums.

The inn has been completely restored to its original grandeur and is decorated with period pieces. Each of the parlors is filled with such amenities as crystal chandeliers, stained glass windows, original fireplaces and ornate plaster ceiling reliefs and moldings.

INNKEEPERS:	Dawn & Albert Schick
ADDRESS:	1853 West Grace Street
	Richmond, Virginia 23220
TELEPHONE:	(804) 353-4334
E-MAIL:	innkeeper@thegracemanorinn.com
WEBSITE:	www.thegracemanorinn.com
ROOMS:	3 Suites; Private baths
CHILDREN:	Children age 18 and older welcome
ANIMALS:	Not allowed; Resident dogs
HANDICAPPED:	Not handicapped accessible
DIETARY NEEDS:	Will accommodate guests' special dietary needs

Striped Omelet

Makes 8 Servings

"This baked, layered omelet creates a stunning visual of red, green and white stripes. It will wow your guests with its beautiful presentation. Serve it with peppered bacon and potato latkes with sour cream and caviar (see recipe on page 175)." - Innkeeper, Grace Manor Inn

13   large eggs, divided
⅜   teaspoon salt, divided
White pepper, to taste
11   tablespoons heavy cream, divided
¼   cup chopped oil-packed sun-dried tomatoes
1   tablespoon finely chopped fresh basil
1   (10-ounce) package frozen chopped spinach, thawed and squeezed dry
¼   cup dried shallots or onions
1½   cups coarsely grated sharp white cheddar cheese

Preheat oven to 450°F. In a bowl, whisk together 4 eggs, ⅛ teaspoon of salt and white pepper. Whisk in 3 tablespoons of cream. Stir in sun-dried tomatoes and basil. In a separate bowl, whisk together 4 eggs, ⅛ teaspoon of salt and white pepper. Whisk in 4 tablespoons of cream. Stir in spinach and dried shallots. In a separate bowl, whisk together 5 eggs, ⅛ teaspoon of salt and white pepper. Whisk in 4 tablespoons of cream. Stir in cheese.

Pour sun-dried tomato mixture into an oiled, non-stick 9x5-inch loaf pan (or a 9-inch round cake pan). Put loaf pan in a larger pan filled with about 1 inch of hot water. Bake for 18-20 minutes, until firm to the touch (about 13 minutes if using a cake pan). Pour spinach mixture over sun-dried tomato layer and bake for 18-20 minutes, until firm to the touch (about 13 minutes if using a cake pan). Pour cheese layer over spinach layer and bake for about 20 minutes, until lightly browned and slightly puffed (about 16 minutes if using a cake pan). Cool omelet in pan on a wire rack for 5 minutes, then turn out omelet onto a long platter. Slice and serve hot, warm or at room temperature.

Ridge View

Ridge View Bed & Breakfast is nestled in Madison County, just north of Charlottesville, on Virginia Byway Route 231 in the Blue Ridge Mountains – one of America's ten most outstanding scenic byways. Ridge View is a beautifully restored farmhouse bed & breakfast, located on 17 rolling acres with views of the Blue Ridge Mountains.

Ridge View is convenient to many historic Virginia and Charlottesville locations, including Monticello, Montpelier and the University of Virginia.

INNKEEPERS:	Eleanor & Frank Damico
ADDRESS:	Scenic Byway 231
	Rochelle, Virginia 22738
TELEPHONE:	(540) 672-7024
E-MAIL:	edamico@virginia-ridgeview.com
WEBSITE:	www.virginia-ridgeview.com
ROOMS:	3 Rooms; Private baths
CHILDREN:	Welcome
ANIMALS:	Dogs welcome; Call ahead; Resident dogs
HANDICAPPED:	Not handicapped accessible
DIETARY NEEDS:	Will accommodate guests' special dietary needs

Potato & Pepper Frittata

Makes 6 to 8 Servings

"This recipe evolved through trial and error." ~ Innkeeper, Ridge View Bed & Breakfast

¼	cup olive oil
1	cup frozen shredded hash browns
1	yellow onion, thinly sliced
½	cup chopped red bell pepper
½	cup chopped green bell pepper
½	cup chopped yellow bell pepper
½	stick butter
8	large eggs

Salt and black pepper, to taste
1   cup grated mozzarella cheese

In a large (10-inch) oven-proof skillet, heat olive oil over medium heat. Add hash browns and cook for 5 minutes. Add onions and red, green and yellow bell peppers; cook until softened. Add butter and cook, stirring, until butter is melted and combined.

Preheat broiler. Beat eggs, salt and pepper; pour over ingredients in skillet. Cook, lifting edges of eggs and letting uncooked egg flow underneath, until eggs are set but still moist, about 10 minutes. Sprinkle frittata with cheese. Transfer skillet to oven and broil for about 5 minutes, until top is set and golden. Carefully loosen edges of frittata and remove to a serving platter. Slice and serve.

Dragon Run Inn

D ragon Run Inn offers yesterday's hospitality coupled with today's conveniences. Enjoy the relaxed atmosphere of a 1913 country farm house. The inn is named for the Dragon Run Swamp, which boasts the largest stand of cypress this far north. The house was built with cypress from the Dragon.

The inn's theme is inspired by the home's roots as a farm, with rooms named for farm animals. Relax in the Jacuzzi and awaken to the aroma of fresh brewed coffee and a homemade country-style breakfast.

INNKEEPERS:	Sue & Ivan Hertzler
ADDRESS:	35 Wares Bridge Road
	Church View, Virginia 23032
TELEPHONE:	(804) 758-5719
E-MAIL:	runninn@oasisonline.com
WEBSITE:	www.dragon-run-inn.com
ROOMS:	3 Rooms; Private baths
CHILDREN:	Welcome
ANIMALS:	Not allowed; Resident outdoor cat
HANDICAPPED:	Not handicapped accessible
DIETARY NEEDS:	Will accommodate guests' special dietary needs

Crab Quiche

Makes 6 Servings

"This delicious quiche freezes well – simply defrost it for one hour and then wrap it in foil and reheat it. You can also easily double this recipe to make two quiches." ~ Innkeeper, Dragon Run Inn

8	ounces crabmeat
½	cup condensed milk or half & half
¼	cup sliced green onions
1	(10¾-ounce) can cream of chicken soup
4	large eggs
2	cups grated cheddar cheese
1	(9-inch) deep-dish pie crust

Preheat oven to 350°F. In a large bowl, combine all ingredients and pour into pie crust. Bake for 1 hour. Cool for 5-10 minutes to let quiche set, then slice and serve.

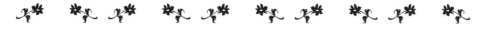

Colonial Gardens

At the Colonial Gardens Bed & Breakfast, wake to the aroma of freshly brewed coffee and meet new friends while you enjoy a full plantation breakfast. Later, sit on the sun porch and enjoy a cool glass of ice tea, or in winter, a cup of hot spiced cider. Guests always return to the gardens and continue to have memorable moments here in Williamsburg.

The romantic, two-room Azalea Suite provides an intimate hideaway. The suite includes a private sitting room and a bedroom with a magnificent rice-carved, four-poster canopy bed and ornate English dresser.

INNKEEPERS:	Scottie & Wil Phillips
ADDRESS:	1109 Jamestown Road
	Williamsburg, Virginia 23185
TELEPHONE:	(757) 220-8087; (800) 886-9715
E-MAIL:	colgdns@widomaker.com
WEBSITE:	www.colonial-gardens.com
ROOMS:	4 Rooms; 2 Suites; Private baths
CHILDREN:	Children age 14 and older welcome
ANIMALS:	Not allowed
HANDICAPPED:	Not handicapped accessible
DIETARY NEEDS:	Will accommodate guests' special dietary needs

Zucchini & Sausage Quiche

Makes 6 Servings

1	large pie crust
½	pound link sausage (removed from casings) or bulk Italian sausage
2	tablespoons butter
2	cups grated or shredded zucchini (about 2 pounds)
1	cup grated Swiss cheese
3	large eggs
1½	cups half & half
¼	cup grated Parmesan cheese
½	teaspoon salt
¼	teaspoon white pepper

Preheat oven to 450°F. Bake pie crust for 8 minutes. Cook and crumble sausage until browned; drain and set aside. Melt 2 tablespoons of butter in a skillet over medium heat. Add zucchini and cook until tender; drain. Spread zucchini over bottom of crust. Sprinkle sausage and Swiss cheese over zucchini.

Lightly beat eggs. Add half & half, Parmesan cheese, salt and white pepper; mix well and pour over ingredients in crust. Bake for 15 minutes. Lower heat to 350°F and bake for 15 minutes more, or until center is almost firm but still cool. Cool for 5-10 minutes to let quiche set, then slice and serve.

Note: You may cook the sausage and zucchini the night before.

Harborton House

Harborton House reflects the charm and warmth of the quaint bayside fishing village of Harborton on the Eastern Shore of Virginia. The inn's destination is central to Assateaque State Park, Chincoteague, NASA, Kiptopeke State Park and Tangier Island. Launch your boat at the public ramp just down the street and be on the Chesapeake Bay in minutes – cruising, fishing, crabbing, exploring or simply anchored enjoying the view.

Enjoy breakfast in the dining room, on the porch or in your room. Then relax on the wrap-around porches or in the lovely, tranquil gardens.

INNKEEPERS:	Helen & Andy Glenn
ADDRESS:	28044 Harborton Road
	Harborton, Virginia 23389
TELEPHONE:	(757) 442-6800
E-MAIL:	info@harbortonhouse.com
WEBSITE:	www.harbortonhouse.com
ROOMS:	2 Rooms; 1 Suite; Private baths
CHILDREN:	Children age 7 and older welcome
ANIMALS:	Not allowed; Resident dog & cat
HANDICAPPED:	Not handicapped accessible
DIETARY NEEDS:	Will accommodate guests' special dietary needs

Tomato Quiche

Makes 6 Servings

1	(9-inch) pie crust
¼	cup all-purpose flour
½	teaspoon salt
⅛	teaspoon black pepper
2	large tomatoes (not too ripe)
2	tablespoons olive oil
1	cup sliced green onions
3	large slices provolone cheese
2	large eggs, beaten
1	cup grated cheddar cheese
1	cup half & half

Preheat oven to 425°F. Bake pie crust for 8 minutes and set aside. Combine flour, salt and pepper. Cut each tomato into 6 (½-inch-thick) slices; dip tomato slices in flour mixture. Heat olive oil over medium heat. Add tomatoes and cook until flour coating is browned slightly.

Lower oven temperature to 375°F. Sprinkle green onions over crust. Top with provolone cheese and tomatoes. Beat eggs, cheddar cheese and half & half; pour over ingredients in crust. Bake for 40-45 minutes, or until set. Cool for 5-10 minutes, then slice and serve.

Barclay Cottage

Built in 1895, Barclay Cottage is one of two remaining Victorian cottages in Virginia Beach. Antiques, hand-made quilts, luxurious robes and plush towels await you. Enjoy a sumptuous, full breakfast of cereal, fruits, baked goods and a hot entrée served in the great room each morning.

After breakfast, head for the beach with complimentary beach chairs, towels, umbrellas and boogie boards. In cooler weather, enjoy whale-watching with scientists from the Virginia Marine Science Museum or explore the many museums and shops in the area.

INNKEEPERS:	Steve & Marie-Louise LaFond
ADDRESS:	400 16th Street
	Virginia Beach, Virginia 23451
TELEPHONE:	(757) 422-1956
E-MAIL:	innkeepers@barclaycottage.com
WEBSITE:	www.barclaycottage.com
ROOMS:	5 Rooms; Private & shared baths
CHILDREN:	Welcome
ANIMALS:	Not allowed; Resident dogs
HANDICAPPED:	Not handicapped accessible
DIETARY NEEDS:	Will accommodate guests' special dietary needs

Rita's Spinach Pie

Makes 10 Servings

"A delicious mixture of cheese and spinach enrobed in a crispy phyllo crust." ~ Innkeeper, Barclay Cottage Bed & Breakfast

2   tablespoons plus 1½ sticks butter
1   large onion, chopped
2   (16-ounce) packages frozen chopped spinach, defrosted and
     squeezed dry
1   (16-ounce) carton small-curd cottage cheese
1   pound feta cheese, crumbled
6   eggs, beaten
¼   cup all-purpose flour
Salt and black pepper, to taste
1   pound phyllo dough

Preheat oven to 350°F. Melt 2 tablespoons of butter in a skillet over medium heat. Add onion and cook until soft. Add spinach and cook until warm. Drain any liquid from skillet. Combine spinach mixture, cottage cheese, feta cheese, eggs and flour. Season with salt and pepper.

Melt the 1½ sticks of butter. With a pastry brush, brush melted butter over bottom of a 12x18-inch baking pan. Working quickly, unfold and separate layers of phyllo dough. Put 6 layers of phyllo in bottom of pan, brushing each layer with melted butter. Spread spinach mixture over layers of phyllo in pan. Top with 6 more sheets of phyllo, brushing each layer with melted butter. Bake for about 30-40 minutes, until golden brown and crisp.

76 Market Street

A Victorian 19th-century inn, 76 Market Street is located in the quiet residential area of Onancock, on Virginia's beautiful Eastern Shore. The inn is just four blocks from the wharf with access to the Chesapeake Bay. Activities include biking, fishing, relaxing, visiting historical sites or taking a ferry to Tangier Island.

Breakfast begins with a baked in-season fruit and then moves on to entrées such as omelets, pancakes, Belgian waffles or one of the inn's specialty dishes. Homemade bread, muffins or scones are also offered.

INNKEEPERS:	Mike & Marge Carpenter
ADDRESS:	76 Market Street
	Onancock, Virginia 23417
TELEPHONE:	(757) 787-7600; (888) 751-7600
E-MAIL:	hosts@76marketst.com
WEBSITE:	www.76marketst.com
ROOMS:	3 Rooms; Private baths
CHILDREN:	Children age 6 and older welcome
ANIMALS:	Not allowed
HANDICAPPED:	Not handicapped accessible
DIETARY NEEDS:	Will accommodate guests' special dietary needs

Main Line Strata

Makes 1 Serving

"This dish is named after the Main Line News, *a Philadelphia newspaper whose travel writer wrote a glowing review of this recipe and his stay at 76 Market Street. The recipe (and our inn) has since also received raves from Chesapeake Bay Magazine. This dish makes one serving – simply multiply for the given number of guests." ~ Innkeeper, 76 Market Street Bed & Breakfast.*

1   slice bread
2   large eggs
1   tablespoon Worcestershire sauce
Pinch of salt
⅓   cup skim milk
½   cup grated cheddar cheese
1   sprig fresh rosemary, for garnish

Preheat oven to 375°F. For each serving, spray an 8-ounce ramekin with non-stick cooking spray. Cut bread into quarters and spread over bottom of ramekin. Whisk eggs, Worcestershire, salt and milk until well combined; pour over bread. Sprinkle with cheese.

Bake for 20-25 minutes, until slightly brown on top. (The cheese will be puffy but will quickly fall, so serve the strata immediately in the ramekin placed on a dinner plate.) Garnish with a sprig of fresh rosemary.

Note: Some guests want to eat this strata right out of the ramekin, others prefer to have it removed – a quick run around the sides of the ramekin with a kitchen knife will allow it to slide out nicely onto a plate.

The Mountain Rose Inn

The Mountain Rose Inn is another example of Old Joe's (Joseph H. DeHart) attention to detail. Designed at the turn of the 20th century in the shape of a "T" with porches along every exterior wall, the house is built of wood cut and dried on the property and bricks made from clay and baked in a kiln specially built to fire them. The house features a metal roof, Victorian embellishments and tongue-and-groove woodwork.

Each morning, by the glow of the oil lamp, breakfast is elegantly served on antique silver and china next to a cozy fire.

INNKEEPERS:	Reeves & Melodie Pogue
ADDRESS:	1787 Charity Highway
	Woolwine, Virginia 24185
TELEPHONE:	(276) 930-1057
E-MAIL:	info@mountainrose-inn.com
WEBSITE:	www.mountainrose-inn.com
ROOMS:	5 Rooms; Private baths
CHILDREN:	Children age 2 and older welcome
ANIMALS:	Not allowed
HANDICAPPED:	Call ahead
DIETARY NEEDS:	Call ahead

Italian Strata

Makes 6 to 8 Servings

"This strata is great for brunch. It is prepared the night before – in the morning, just pop it in the oven!" ~ Innkeeper, The Mountain Rose Inn

12 slices bread (crusts removed), cut into 1-inch pieces
1 (16-ounce) package mild or spicy bulk sausage
1 cup chopped green bell pepper
½ cup chopped onion
1½ cups grated cheese (pizza or Italian blend work well)
1 teaspoon dried oregano
1 teaspoon dried basil
7 large eggs
1 tablespoon dry mustard
3 cups milk
5 slices tomato, cut in half
Grated Parmesan cheese

Grease a 9x13-inch baking dish. Spread bread over bottom of baking dish, cutting to fit as needed. Cook sausage in a skillet over medium heat until cooked through; drain. In a large bowl, combine sausage, bell pepper, onion, the 1½ cups of grated cheese, oregano and basil; spread over bread cubes.

In a bowl or a blender, combine eggs, dry mustard and milk; mix well. Pour egg mixture over sausage mixture. Cover with tomato slices. Sprinkle with Parmesan cheese. Cover and refrigerate overnight.

The next day, bring strata to room temperature. Preheat oven to 350°F. Bake strata for 1 hour, or until completely set. Let stand for 5 minutes, then slice and serve.

Summerfield Inn

S ummerfield Inn, built in 1921 for the family of a local lumber dealer, offers seven elegant, individually decorated guestrooms, all with private baths (five with whirlpools). The inn is furnished with elegant American and European antique furnishings.

There are spacious parlors, sitting areas and a library. A large wrap-around porch with swing and rocking chairs draws you outside to relax and enjoy the beautiful gardens and roses.

INNKEEPERS:	Janice & Jim Cowan
ADDRESS:	101 West Valley Street
	Abingdon, Virginia 24210
TELEPHONE:	(276) 628-5905; (800) 688-5905
E-MAIL:	stay@summerfieldinn.com
WEBSITE:	www.summerfieldinn.com
ROOMS:	7 Rooms; Private baths
CHILDREN:	Children age 12 and older welcome
ANIMALS:	Not allowed
HANDICAPPED:	Not handicapped accessible
DIETARY NEEDS:	Will accommodate guests' special dietary needs

Pesto Strata

Makes 1 Serving

"A Mediterranean-style dish with plenty of flavor. Sumptuous aromas will fill the air. For the daring, Greek olives can be added. It makes one serving – simply multiply for the desired number of servings. Plan ahead, this dish needs to be started the night before." ~ Innkeeper, Summerfield Inn Bed & Breakfast

1 cup cubed sun-dried tomato bread (about 1-2 slices of bread)
⅛ teaspoon dried pesto seasoning
Salt and black pepper, to taste
2 tablespoons crumbled feta cheese
Greek olives, pitted and sliced (optional)
1 large egg
⅓ cup milk

Spray a 10-ounce ramekin with non-stick cooking spray. Layer bread in ramekin. Top with pesto seasoning, salt, pepper, feta cheese and olives. Whisk together egg and milk; pour over ingredients in ramekin. Cover and refrigerate overnight.

The next day, let strata stand at room temperature for 30 minutes. Preheat oven to 375°F. Bake for 20-25 minutes, until set.

The Inn at Monticello

Guests find the Inn at Monticello a quiet place to relax and enjoy time away from their fast-paced lives. In winter, fireplaces offer soothing places to read or just unwind. Summer finds most guests on the porch in a rocking chair enjoying a cool drink. Enjoy a walk to picturesque Willow Lake adjacent to the inn, or a game of croquet or bocce.

In the Green Room, the high, carved headboard of the antique, queen-size bed with matching furniture dates to the late 1800s. A sitting area near the wood-burning fireplace offers the comfort and elegance of years gone by.

INNKEEPERS:	Norm & Becky Lindway
ADDRESS:	Route 20 South, 1188 Scottsville Road
	Charlottesville, Virginia 22902
TELEPHONE:	(434) 979-3593
E-MAIL:	stay@innatmonticello.com
WEBSITE:	www.innatmonticello.com
ROOMS:	5 Rooms; 1 Suite; Private baths
CHILDREN:	Children age 12 and older welcome
ANIMALS:	Not allowed; Resident cat
HANDICAPPED:	Not handicapped accessible
DIETARY NEEDS:	Will accommodate guests' special dietary needs

Fiesta Veggie Bake

Makes 12 Servings

1   sheet puff pastry
1   cup chopped ham or cooked crumbled sausage (optional)
1   tablespoon butter
½   large green bell pepper, diced
6   green onions, sliced
8   ounces mushrooms, sliced
¼   pound asparagus or broccoli, chopped
8   large eggs
½   cup half & half
1   (16-ounce) package Fiesta shredded potatoes (hash browns with Mexican seasonings)
2   cups grated mild cheddar cheese
Sliced fresh tomato, for serving
Sour cream, for serving

Preheat oven to 350°F. Spray a 9x13-inch baking dish with non-stick cooking spray. Roll out puff pastry until thin enough to cover bottom and 1 inch up sides of baking dish. Melt butter in a skillet over medium heat. Add bell pepper, green onions, mushrooms and asparagus or broccoli; cook until vegetables are soft. In a large bowl, beat eggs and half & half.

Spread potatoes over puff pastry. Sprinkle with ham or sausage. Sprinkle with mushroom mixture and grated cheese. Pour egg mixture over all. Bake for 40-45 minutes, until eggs are set. Serve with tomato slices and a dollop of sour cream.

Colonial Capital

C olonial Capital Bed & Breakfast was established in 1988. A complete renovation of this 1926 Colonial Revival home retained its elegance, graciousness and Southern gentility. A rich blend of warmth, style and comfort enhance the antique furnishings and Oriental rugs which highlight the décor. Cozy canopied beds, a full breakfast, delightful innkeepers, a charming home and a fascinating area are hallmarks of this escape.

Colonial Capital was among the 25 proud recipients of the first annual "America's Favorite Inns, B&B's and Small Hotels" award.

INNKEEPERS:	Barbara & Phil Craig
ADDRESS:	501 Richmond Road
	Williamsburg, Virginia 23185
TELEPHONE:	(757) 229-0233; (800) 776-0570
E-MAIL:	ccbb@widomaker.com
WEBSITE:	www.ccbb.com
ROOMS:	5 Rooms; 1 Suite; Private baths
CHILDREN:	Children age 8 and older welcome
ANIMALS:	Not allowed
HANDICAPPED:	Not handicapped accessible
DIETARY NEEDS:	Will accommodate guests' special dietary needs

Hearty Breakfast Soufflé

Makes 4 to 6 Servings

Plan ahead, this dish needs to be started the night before serving.

12 slices coarse-grained white bread, crusts removed
6 thin slices American cheese
6 thin slices Virginia ham
6 thin slices Swiss cheese
4 large eggs, slightly beaten
½ teaspoon dry mustard
2 cups milk
5⅓ tablespoons butter or margarine, melted
⅔ cup crushed corn flakes
Melon slices or grapes clusters, for garnish

Grease a 9x13-inch glass baking dish. Arrange 4 slices of bread in corners of baking dish and 4 half-slices of bread in middle of dish. Top bread with American cheese, ham and Swiss cheese. Layer remaining 6 slices of bread in the same arrangement as the first 6 slices. In a medium bowl, beat eggs and dry mustard. Beat in milk and pour over ingredients in baking dish. Cover and refrigerate overnight.

The next day, preheat oven to 350°F. Pour butter evenly over ingredients in baking dish. Sprinkle with corn flakes. Bake for 55-60 minutes, or until slightly browned and puffed. Cut into 4-6 slices and serve immediately. Garnish with melon slices or clusters of grapes.

Applewood Inn

Conveniently located midway between Lexington and Natural Bridge at the upper end of a long hollow which follows scenic Buffalo Creek, Applewood Inn Bed & Breakfast and its 37 acres is perched high above the creek in a very private and beautiful setting.

This passive solar home is furnished with antiques, reproductions, quilts and original artwork with massive lodge-style, south-facing porches that afford lovely views of the surrounding woods, hillside pastures with grazing llamas and the distant mountains.

INNKEEPERS:	Linda & Christian Best
ADDRESS:	Tarn Beck Lane off Buffalo Bend Road
	Lexington, Virginia 24450
TELEPHONE:	(540) 463-1962; (800) 463-1902
E-MAIL:	inn@applewoodbb.com
WEBSITE:	www.applewoodbb.com
ROOMS:	4 Rooms; Private baths
CHILDREN:	Children age 6 and older welcome
ANIMALS:	Dogs allowed in 1 Room; Resident dogs & cat
HANDICAPPED:	Call ahead
DIETARY NEEDS:	Will accommodate guests' special dietary needs

Breakfast Casserole

Makes 6 Servings

"This casserole is particularly good when our garden asparagus is in season. If I have a guest who is a vegetarian, I simply bake the dish in individual ramekins and leave out the meat in the necessary number of servings." ~ Innkeeper, Applewood Inn & Llama Trekking

1	tablespoon butter or olive oil
1	cup chopped red bell pepper
1	cup chopped asparagus (or broccoli)
¾	cup sliced mushrooms
1-2	green onions, sliced
3	cups grated potatoes (or defrosted frozen hash browns)
½	cup chopped ham or cooked crumbled sausage
¼	cup crumbled goat cheese
6	large eggs
3	tablespoons milk
¾	teaspoon salt
½	teaspoon black pepper
1	teaspoon dried thyme
⅛	teaspoon dry mustard
1¼	cups grated sharp cheddar cheese

Preheat oven to 400°F. Melt butter in a skillet over medium heat. Add bell pepper, asparagus, mushrooms and green onions; cook for 5 minutes, stirring occasionally, until softened. Transfer asparagus mixture to a large bowl. Add potatoes and ham or sausage; stir to combine, then spread in an 8x8-inch baking dish. Sprinkle with goat cheese.

Beat eggs, milk, salt, pepper, thyme and dry mustard; pour over ingredients in baking dish. Sprinkle with cheddar cheese. Bake for 20 minutes. Lower oven temperature to 375°F and bake for about 15-20 minutes more, until eggs are set.

Victoria & Albert Inn

The Victoria & Albert Inn, an elegant 1892 Victorian home, was restored in 1987. It is an award-winning inn recognized nationally for its five beautiful guest rooms with antique furnishings, whirlpool tubs, fireplaces and more.

A full breakfast includes specialities such as mushroom cheese omelet and Belgian waffles topped with fresh fruit and whipped cream, served with hot, freshly baked biscuits and breads.

INNKEEPERS:	Hazel Ramos-Cano & Richard Cano
ADDRESS:	224 Oak Hill Street
	Abingdon, Virginia 24210
TELEPHONE:	(276) 623-1281
E-MAIL:	rcano@naxs.com
WEBSITE:	www.abingdon-virginia.com
ROOMS:	4 Rooms; 1 Suite; Private baths
CHILDREN:	Children age 12 and older welcome
ANIMALS:	Not allowed
HANDICAPPED:	Not handicapped accessible
DIETARY NEEDS:	Will accommodate guests' special dietary needs

Brunch Egg Nachos

Makes 4 Servings

"During spring race weekend and summer NASCAR race weekend, when our guests are big eaters and energy burners, this is a crowd pleaser." ~ Innkeeper, Victoria & Albert Inn

½ pound bulk pork sausage
1 small onion, chopped
1 (4-ounce) can diced green chilies
4 cups crisp-fried tortillas (fresh flour tortillas cut into triangles and fried in a little oil or deep-fried)
2 cups grated mild cheddar or jack cheese, divided
4-8 large eggs (1-2 eggs per person)

Condiments:
½ cup each: sour cream, guacamole, sliced green onions, sliced black olives and taco sauce

Preheat broiler. In a skillet over medium-high heat, combine sausage and onions. Cook, crumbling sausage, until sausage is browned and onions are translucent; drain grease. Stir in chilies and set aside. Divide fried tortillas among 4 shallow ramekins or oven-proof bowls. Distribute sausage mixture evenly over tortillas. Top sausage in each ramekin with ¼ cup of cheese.

Poach or fry eggs; add 1-2 eggs to each ramekin. Top eggs in each ramekin with ¼ cup of cheese. Put ramekins on a baking sheet and broil, 6 inches from heat, until cheese is melted. Put each ramekin on a salad plate lined with a doily. Put condiments in small bowls and pass down the table.

Side Dishes

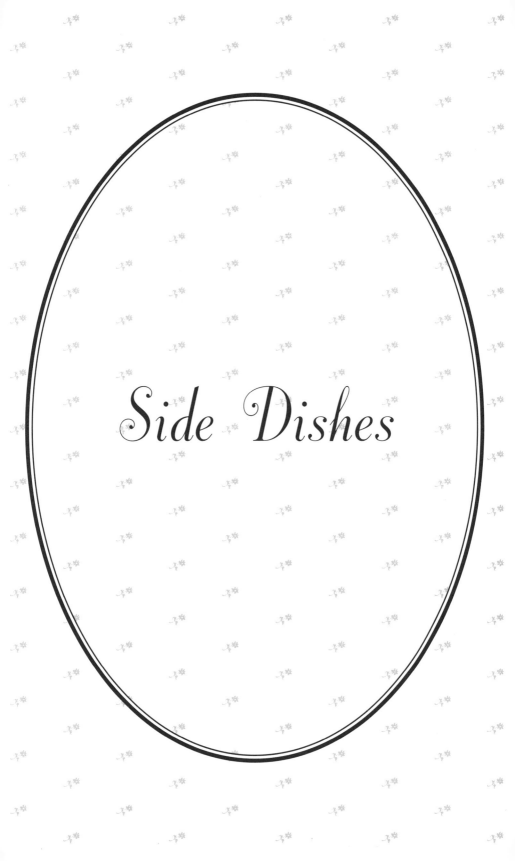

Side Dishes

76 Market Street

Guest rooms at 76 Market Street Bed & Breakfast are spacious and the beds have nice firm mattresses topped with feather beds. With easy access by car or boat, the inn is in an ideal spot for activities on the Eastern Shore from Chincoteague to Cape Charles.

"Every experience, both in the B&B and in town, was exceptional. The level of service and genuine friendliness was unexpected. Hope to come back soon. Contact us when you decide to publish a cookbook – the breakfasts were great!" ~ Guest, 76 Market Street

INNKEEPERS:	Mike & Marge Carpenter
ADDRESS:	76 Market Street
	Onancock, Virginia 23417
TELEPHONE:	(757) 787-7600; (888) 751-7600
E-MAIL:	hosts@76MarketSt.com
WEBSITE:	www.76MarketSt.com
ROOMS:	3 Rooms; Private baths
CHILDREN:	Children age 6 and older welcome
ANIMALS:	Not allowed
HANDICAPPED:	Not handicapped accessible
DIETARY NEEDS:	Will accommodate guests' special dietary needs

Baked Grits with Sausage

Makes 12 Servings

"We provide recipes of the dishes we serve, but with this one we do not reveal the main ingredient (grits) until (most) everyone has had seconds. It is fun to watch our Northern friends when they find out they do actually like grits!" ~ Innkeeper, 76 Market Street Bed & Breakfast

3¾   cups water
1   cup regular old-fashioned or quick grits (not instant grits)
1   teaspoon salt
1   cup grated cheddar cheese, divided
½   teaspoon garlic salt
1   stick butter plus divided
12   ounces bulk sausage, crumbled and browned
2   large eggs, well beaten
¼   cup skim milk
¼   teaspoon salt
Pinch of cayenne pepper
1   cup crushed corn flakes

Preheat oven to 350°F. Spray an 8x11-inch glass baking dish with non-stick cooking spray. Bring water to a boil, add grits and cook, stirring occasionally at first and nearly constantly at the end, until done, about 7 minutes. Add salt, ¾ cup of cheese, garlic salt, ½ stick of butter and sausage; mix well until butter is melted and combined. Cool grits mixture.

Combine eggs, milk, salt and cayenne pepper; add to grits and stir to combine well. Pour grits into baking dish. Melt the remaining ½ stick of butter and combine with corn flakes and the remaining ¼ cup of cheese; sprinkle over grits mixture. Bake for 40-45 minutes. Let stand for at least 20 minutes before serving.

Note: This dish can be made a day ahead (up to the baking step), covered and refrigerated.

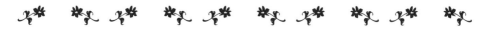

Inn on Town Creek

The Inn on Town Creek, one of the area's finest country inns, is a short walk to downtown Abingdon, home of the world-famous Barter Theatre, the William King Art Center, the Virginia Creeper Trail and adjacent to the Mount Rogers National Recreation Area. Seasonally, you can attend NASCAR events in nearby Bristol, Tennessee, the renowned Virginia Highlands Festival, the Mistletoe Market and the Garden Faire.

The inn has two suites that include kitchens and private entrances onto covered porches.

INNKEEPERS:	Dr. Roger & Linda Neal
ADDRESS:	445 East Valley Street
	Abingdon, Virginia 24212
TELEPHONE:	(276) 628-4560
E-MAIL:	lindaneal@naxs.net
WEBSITE:	www.innontowncreek.com
ROOMS:	5 Rooms; 2 Suites; Private & shared baths
CHILDREN:	Children age 6 and older welcome; Call ahead
ANIMALS:	Welcome; call ahead
HANDICAPPED:	Not handicapped accessible
DIETARY NEEDS:	Will accommodate guests' special dietary needs

Breakfast Grits

Makes 10 Servings

"I usually make a quadruple batch of grits and freeze them in one-quart freezer bags to use as needed." ~ Innkeeper, Inn on Town Creek

6	cups water
2	cups white or yellow grits
1	teaspoon salt plus extra, to taste
1	clove garlic, minced (or granulated garlic, to taste)
1-2	tablespoons finely minced onion (optional)
1	stick butter
½	cup milk
3	cups grated cheddar cheese
4	large eggs, slightly beaten
1	teaspoon hot pepper sauce

Black pepper, to taste

Preheat oven to 350°F. Butter a 2-quart casserole dish. Bring water to a boil in a large saucepan. Add grits and 1 teaspoon of salt. Lower heat, cover and simmer for 25-30 minutes, stirring occasionally, until done (add garlic and onion during last 5 minutes of cooking time). Add butter, milk, cheese, eggs and hot sauce; stir until cheese is melted and combined. Season with salt and pepper. Pour grits into casserole dish. Bake for 45-50 minutes.

Bennett House

B ennett House Bed & Breakfast has been faithfully restored in the tradition in which it was built. The bedrooms offer comfortable, antique brass four-poster beds and air conditioning. Wine and cheese or tea are available when you check in. Relax in the hot tub, lounge on the inn's porches or on the patio, or simply stroll the inn's lawns.

Breakfast is a full Virginia-style country breakfast which consists of one of several unique breakfast dishes ranging from simple country eggs and sausage to more sophisticated creations.

INNKEEPERS:	Jean & Curtis Harrover
ADDRESS:	9252 Bennett Drive
	Manassas, Virginia 20110
TELEPHONE:	(703) 368-6121; (800) 354-7060
E-MAIL:	jharrover@aol.com
WEBSITE:	www.virginia-bennetthouse.com
ROOMS:	2 Rooms; Private baths
CHILDREN:	Children age 5 and older welcome
ANIMALS:	Not allowed; Resident pets
HANDICAPPED:	Not handicapped accessible
DIETARY NEEDS:	Will accommodate guests' special dietary needs

Breakfast Sausage Loaf

Makes 4 Servings

"Guest rave about this dish." ~ Innkeeper, Bennett House Bed & Breakfast

1   (16-ounce) package Jimmy Dean regular sausage
1   (16-ounce) package Jimmy Dean hot sausage
1   large egg, lightly beaten
1   cup finely chopped peeled apple
½   cup chopped onion
¾   cup cracker crumbs
½   cup packed brown sugar
½   teaspoon liquid smoke

Preheat oven to 350°F. Mix all ingredients as for a meatloaf. Shape into a large loaf and place in a 9x5-inch loaf pan. Bake for 75 minutes, until loaf is firm and cooked through. The loaf may be frozen after it has cooled.

Dragon Run Inn

The Dragon Run Inn is ideally located for day trips. Within an hour, you can be shopping the Williamsburg outlet stores or walking the streets of historic Williamsburg, Jamestown or Yorktown. Richmond is an hour away, as are Water Country, Busch Gardens and Kings Dominion. Colonial Downs is also close by for an evening with the horses.

If you like to canoe, the Dragon Run Swamp calls. The Dragon is considered to be one of the most pristine bodies of water in the East – it is a naturalist's paradise, with a number of unusual species of plants, animals and aquatic life.

INNKEEPERS:	Sue & Ivan Hertzler
ADDRESS:	35 Wares Bridge Road
	Church View, Virginia 23032
TELEPHONE:	(804) 758-5719
E-MAIL:	runninn@oasisonline.com
WEBSITE:	www.dragon-run-inn.com
ROOMS:	3 Rooms; Private baths
CHILDREN:	Welcome
ANIMALS:	Not allowed; Resident outdoor cat
HANDICAPPED:	Not handicapped accessible
DIETARY NEEDS:	Will accommodate guests' special dietary needs

Sausage Loaf

Makes 2 Loaves

Favorite fresh or frozen bread dough (enough for 2 loaves)
½   pound mild bulk pork sausage
½   pound hot bulk pork sausage
1½   cups chopped fresh mushrooms
½   cup chopped onion
3   large eggs
2½   cups grated mozzarella cheese
1   teaspoon dried basil
1   teaspoon dried parsley flakes
1   teaspoon garlic powder
1   teaspoon dried crushed rosemary
¼   teaspoon dried thyme

Preheat oven to 350°F. Prepare bread dough and let rise until nearly doubled in size. Cook and crumble sausage in a skillet over medium heat until nearly done. Add mushrooms and onion; cook, stirring, until sausage is browned and vegetables are tender. Drain sausage mixture, then set aside to cool. Beat 2 eggs and add to cooled sausage mixture along with cheese, basil, parsley, garlic powder, rosemary and thyme; mix well.

Punch down dough and roll each piece into a 12x16-inch rectangle. Spread ½ of sausage mixture over each rectangle to within 1 inch of edges. Roll up dough jelly roll-style, starting at the narrow end. Seal edges and put loaves on a greased baking sheet. Bake for 25 minutes. Beat remaining 1 egg and brush over tops of loaves. Bake for 5-10 minutes more, until golden brown.

Grace Manor Inn

The Grace Manor Inn has large, two-room suites with luxurious private baths, a formal dining room, a sunroom and three formal parlors. The parlors are filled with such amenities as original Tiffany chandeliers, stained glass windows, crystal chandeliers and ornate plaster ceiling reliefs and moldings.

In 1996, Grace Manor was awarded a Certificate for Historic Preservation by the United States Department of Interior and is listed on the National and State Registers of Historic Places.

INNKEEPERS:	Dawn & Albert Schick
ADDRESS:	1853 West Grace Street
	Richmond, Virginia 23220
TELEPHONE:	(804) 353-4334
E-MAIL:	innkeeper@thegracemanorinn.com
WEBSITE:	www.thegracemanorinn.com
ROOMS:	3 Suites; Private baths
CHILDREN:	Children age 18 and older welcome
ANIMALS:	Not allowed; Resident dogs
HANDICAPPED:	Not handicapped accessible
DIETARY NEEDS:	Will accommodate guests' special dietary needs

Potato Latkes with Sour Cream & Caviar

Makes 4 Servings

"This dish, which is adapted from the cookbook Barefoot Contessa Parties, *is always a favorite with our guests. There is something so decadent about pairing sour cream and caviar with freshly prepared potato latkes. Our motto is "Let us pamper you," and guests most definitely feel pampered after enjoying such a treat." ~ Innkeeper, Grace Manor Inn*

6	cups grated or shredded potatoes
2	extra-large eggs, beaten
6	tablespoons all-purpose flour
1	onion, chopped
2½	teaspoons kosher salt
½	teaspoon black pepper
3	tablespoons butter
3	tablespoons olive oil
½	cup sour cream
3¼	ounces caviar (optional)

Put potatoes in a colander or kitchen towel and squeeze out as much liquid as possible. Combine potatoes, eggs, flour, onion, salt and pepper; mix well. Melt 1 tablespoon of butter with 1 tablespoon of olive oil in a skillet over medium heat. Add potato mixture to skillet using 1½ tablespoons of potato mixture per latke. Flatten latkes with a spatula and cook for 2 minutes. Turn, flatten again and cook for 2 minutes more, or until crisp and golden brown. Repeat with remaining potato mixture, butter and oil. Serve latkes with separate dishes of sour cream and caviar.

South River Country Inn

G uests of South River Country Inn enjoy strolling around the farm to visit with the cows and chickens or fishing in one of the stocked ponds. Whether you prefer lounging in the hammock or taking in the sights nearby, there is always something for everyone to do, including hiking, horseback riding, canoeing, tubing, skiing, antiquing or spending the day touring some of the local wineries or historical sites.

From the moment you arrive, you will feel at home. You will awake from a peaceful night's sleep to a hearty and delicious country-style breakfast.

INNKEEPERS:	Judy & Cliff Braun
ADDRESS:	3011 South River Road
	Stanardsville, Virginia 22973
TELEPHONE:	(434) 985-2901; (877) 874-4473
E-MAIL:	cbraun@sprintmail.com
WEBSITE:	www.southrivercountryinn.com
ROOMS:	3 Rooms; 1 Suite; 1 Cottage; Private baths
CHILDREN:	Children age 6 and older welcome
ANIMALS:	Not allowed; Resident outdoor dog
HANDICAPPED:	Not handicapped accessible
DIETARY NEEDS:	Will accommodate guests' special dietary needs

Hash Brown Casserole

Makes 10 Servings

"A favorite of our military men!" ~ *Innkeeper, South River Country Inn*

1   (32-ounce) package frozen shredded hash browns, thawed
1   (10¾-ounce) can cream of celery soup
1   (16-ounce) container sour cream
1   cup grated cheddar cheese
5   tablespoons butter, softened
Tabasco sauce, a few drops or to taste
1   tablespoon Mrs. Dash seasoning

Preheat oven to 325°F. Combine all ingredients and spread in a greased 9x13-inch baking dish. Bake for about 45 minutes.

The Love House

The Love House Bed & Breakfast is a Colonial-style home built in 1850 and lovingly renovated, retaining its original charm. The inn has four beautiful rooms, each with a gas-log fireplace and a private bath with a Jacuzzi tub.

The Dunn Room is decorated in Pompeian red, burgundy, pink and green. The comfortable, queen-size Windsor bed is complemented by a huge armoire, cheval mirror, bureau and secretaire, all in hardwood cherry.

INNKEEPERS:	Hazel Ramos-Cano & Richard Cano
ADDRESS:	210 East Valley Street
	Abingdon, Virginia 24210
TELEPHONE:	(276) 623-1281
E-MAIL:	lovehouse@naxs.com
WEBSITE:	www.abingdon-virginia.com
ROOMS:	2 Rooms; 2 Suites; Private baths
CHILDREN:	Children age 12 and older welcome
ANIMALS:	Not allowed
HANDICAPPED:	Not handicapped accessible
DIETARY NEEDS:	Will accommodate guests' special dietary needs

Potato Breakfast Fritters

Makes 8 Servings

"Whenever I plan my breakfasts, I try to make sure that I have different colors, shapes and textures incorporated into the meal. This recipe is offered for the crisp texture, the golden color and the round shape." - Innkeeper, The Love House Bed & Breakfast

4	large russet potatoes, peeled and quartered
½	large onion
1	tablespoon cornstarch
1	large egg

Salt and black pepper, to taste
2   tablespoons vegetable oil plus more, as needed

Preheat oven to 200°F. Coarsely chop potatoes and onion in a food processor or by hand; transfer to a bowl. Add cornstarch, egg, salt and pepper; mix well. Heat oil in a large skillet over medium heat. Add potatoes and form small patties; cook until golden brown on each side. Keep cooked fritters warm in oven until serving.

The Claiborne House

The Claiborne House Bed & Breakfast is a beautifully restored circa 1895 Queen Anne in the heart of the quiet historic district of Rocky Mount. History envelops the towns of southwest Virginia like the haze that brands the Blue Ridge Mountains. From Rocky Mount, you can pursue it all, from museums to mountains, hiking to scenic highways, antiquing to wine tasting and even toe-tapping, fiddle-playing Bluegrass music.

Stroll the lovely English gardens, complete with fountains and a three-level pond or take in the scenery from the inn's 130-foot-long porch.

INNKEEPERS:	Tony & Shellie Leete
ADDRESS:	185 Claiborne Avenue
	Rocky Mount, Virginia 24151
TELEPHONE:	(540) 483-4616
E-MAIL:	innkeeper@claibornehouse.net
WEBSITE:	www.claibornehouse.net
ROOMS:	5 Rooms; Private baths
CHILDREN:	Children age 12 and older welcome
ANIMALS:	Not allowed
HANDICAPPED:	Not handicapped accessible
DIETARY NEEDS:	Will accommodate guests' special dietary needs

Beans Billabong

Makes 8 Servings

"Who'll come waltzing Matilda with me. Once a jolly swagman camped by a billabong, under the shade of a coolibah tree. And he sang as he watched and waited till his billy boiled. Who'll come a-waltzing Matilda with me. Waltzing Matilda, Waltzing Matilda, who'll come a-waltzing Matilda with me. And he sang as he watched and waited till his billy boiled. Who'll come a-waltzing Matilda with me." ~ Innkeeper, The Historic Claiborne House

6 slices bacon
2 cloves garlic, minced
5 cups fresh green beans, trimmed or 4 (8-ounce) cans green beans
¾ cup grated or shredded Parmesan cheese
Black pepper, to taste

Cook bacon in a large skillet over medium heat until crisp. Remove bacon, cool, crumble and set aside. Drain most of bacon grease, leaving a generous coating in skillet. Add garlic and cook until it begins to brown slightly. Stir in green beans and cook for 5-8 minutes, until they start to turn color. Stir in cheese. Season with pepper. Add bacon and toss to combine. Serve hot.

Appetizers & Salads

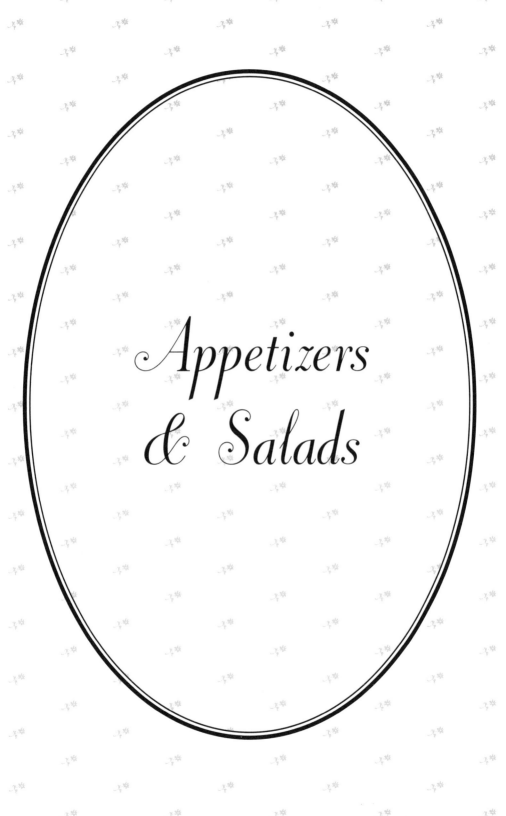

Appetizers
& Salads

The Black Horse Inn

The Black Horse Inn, circa 1850, is named after the Black Horse Cavalry which was conceived at a gathering of Warrenton lawyers in 1858. It was one of the local companies called to active duty by Governor Henry Wise in 1859.

The Black Horse Cavalry led a successful charge against Union forces at the first Battle of Manassas, winning the special praise of Confederate President Jefferson Davis. Following the war, a number of the men from the Black Horse became prominent leaders in the Commonwealth.

INNKEEPERS:	Lynn Pirozzoli
ADDRESS:	8393 Meetze Road
	Warrenton, Virginia 20187
TELEPHONE:	(540) 349-4020
E-MAIL:	relax@blackhorseinn.com
WEBSITE:	www.blackhorseinn.com
ROOMS:	8 Rooms; 1 Suite; Private baths
CHILDREN:	Children age 12 and older welcome
ANIMALS:	Horses welcome (overnight stabling); Resident dog
HANDICAPPED:	Not handicapped accessible
DIETARY NEEDS:	Will accommodate guests' special dietary needs

Cucumber, Smoked Salmon & Watercress Sandwiches

Makes 12 (2-inch) Round Tea Sandwiches

"These savory tea sandwiches, trimmed with watercress, will charm your guests." ~ Innkeeper, The Black Horse Inn

½   (8-ounce) package cream cheese, softened
3   tablespoons finely chopped peeled cucumber
3   ounces Nova Scotia smoked salmon, thinly sliced
1   teaspoon plus ½ cup minced, trimmed watercress
½   teaspoon lemon juice
⅛   teaspoon salt
⅛   teaspoon cayenne pepper
12   slices whole-wheat bread, crusts removed
3   tablespoons butter or margarine, softened

In a food processor, process cream cheese until smooth, stopping once to scrape down sides of bowl. Add cucumber, smoked salmon, 1 teaspoon of minced watercress, lemon juice, salt and cayenne; process until well blended.

Cut 2 rounds out of each slice of bread with a 2-inch biscuit cutter or a glass. Spread cream cheese mixture evenly on ½ of bread rounds. Top with remaining bread rounds. Carefully spread edges of sandwiches with butter. Dip edges of sandwiches in remaining ½ cup of watercress to coat. Cover and chill, then serve.

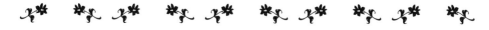

Tree Streets Inn

Located in the beautiful "Crossroads of the Shenandoah Valley," where the Skyline Drive and the Blue Ridge Parkway meet, the Tree Streets Inn offers a soothing getaway in this most beautiful part of Virginia. The 1914 Colonial Revival home welcomes you with warmth and hospitality.

Upon entering, guests are embraced by a spectacular, sweeping "Bridal Staircase." The library and great room call you to relax and read a book, play a game of chess or just enjoy the casual elegance of antiques and turn-of-the-century furnishings.

INNKEEPERS:	William & Nickie Aldridge
ADDRESS:	421 Walnut Avenue
	Waynesboro, Virginia 22980
TELEPHONE:	(540) 949-4484; (877) 378-0456
E-MAIL:	treestreetsinn@ntelos.net
WEBSITE:	www.treestreetsinn.com
ROOMS:	3 Rooms; 1 Suite; Private baths
CHILDREN:	Children age 8 and older welcome
ANIMALS:	Not allowed; Resident dog
HANDICAPPED:	Not handicapped accessible
DIETARY NEEDS:	Will accommodate guests' special dietary needs

Salmon Paste for Tea Sandwiches or Canapés

Makes 10 to 12 Servings

"This old Victorian recipe is easy to prepare and is spread between pieces of rye or white bread. This filling can be used any number of ways – it is excellent served with crackers." - Innkeeper, Tree Streets Inn Bed & Breakfast

1	(8-ounce) package cream cheese, softened
1	(8-ounce) can red salmon, drained (skin and bones removed)
2	tablespoons minced onion
2	tablespoons chopped stuffed olives
1	tablespoon minced fresh parsley
2	teaspoons lemon juice
1	tablespoon Worcestershire sauce
½	teaspoon dried tarragon (or 1½ teaspoons minced fresh tarragon)

Butter, softened
24 slices thin dark rye or white bread, crusts removed

Combine all ingredients in a mixing bowl, except butter and bread. Spread butter on 1 side of each slice of bread, then spread with salmon mixture. Cut into triangles or finger sandwiches. Serve immediately.

Note: If you are not using the salmon paste immediately, cover tightly with a well dampened tea towel, then wrap in plastic wrap and refrigerate.

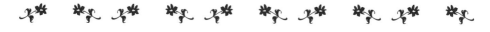

Freemason Inn

S tep back in time to cobblestone streets, quiet neighborhoods, tree-lined walks and breathtaking sunsets, and you'll be at the Freemason Inn Bed & Breakfast. The inn was completely renovated by a distinguished English designer as a turn-of-the-century Victorian home, located in the historic Freemason District of downtown Norfolk.

The inn is surrounded by history, entertainment and culture. The Chrysler Museum, MacArthur Memorial, USS Wisconsin and Nauticus are nearby, as are the symphony, opera and the Virginia Stage Company.

INNKEEPERS:	Robert Epstein & Jonathan Epstein
ADDRESS:	411 West York Street
	Norfolk, Virginia 23510
TELEPHONE:	(866) 388-1897
E-MAIL:	info@freemasoninn.com
WEBSITE:	www.freemasoninn.com
ROOMS:	4 Suites; Private baths
CHILDREN:	Children age 12 and older welcome
ANIMALS:	Not allowed
HANDICAPPED:	Not handicapped accessible
DIETARY NEEDS:	Will accommodate guests' special dietary needs

Chesapeake Bay English Muffins

Makes 8-12 Servings

"Virginia's nutrient-rich Chesapeake Bay offers fine blue fin crabmeat. This appetizer freezes well for last-minute company." ~ Innkeeper, Freemason Inn

¾   stick butter, softened
½   pound blue fin crabmeat
1   (6½-ounce) jar Kraft Old English cheese
1½ teaspoons seasoning salt
½   teaspoon garlic salt
6   English muffins, split

Preheat broiler. Combine all ingredients, except English muffins. Spread English muffin halves evenly with crab mixture (about 1 heaping tablespoon per muffin half). Cut each English muffin half into fourths. Place muffin halves on a baking sheet and broil for 3 minutes.

Note: To freeze muffins, place unbroiled muffin halves on a baking sheet, quick-freeze for about 30 minutes, then store in freezer bags. When ready to use, defrost muffins for 30 minutes before broiling.

South Court Inn

I nnkeepers Anita and Tom Potts spent three years updating and renovating this circa 1870 house to the high Victorian-style typical of the turn of the century. The innkeepers' goal was to create a warm, inviting, luxurious atmosphere for people wanting to get away from the stress of everyday life, where they could feel pampered, yet comfortable.

The Emma Glenn Bedroom boasts a four-poster bed with wood canopy and lace drapery under an antique crystal chandelier. The enclosed claw-foot tub in the large private bath invites guests to take a lingering soak.

INNKEEPERS:	Anita & Tom Potts
ADDRESS:	160 South Court Street
	Luray, Virginia 22835
TELEPHONE:	(540) 843-0980; (888) 749-8055
E-MAIL:	inn@southcourtinn.com
WEBSITE:	www.southcourtinn.com
ROOMS:	3 Rooms; Private baths
CHILDREN:	Children age 12 and older welcome; 1 per room
ANIMALS:	Not allowed
HANDICAPPED:	Not handicapped accessible
DIETARY NEEDS:	Call ahead

Warm Apple Tart with Blue Cheese

Makes 4 Servings

"This dish mimics a great appetizer served at the famed L'Auberge Chez François in Great Falls, Virginia. As we have a large collection of turkeys and ironstone dishes featuring turkey decorations throughout the house, we use a 5-inch cookie cutter in the shape of a turkey to cut the crust for each tart." - Innkeeper, South Court Inn

Dough for 1 pie crust (homemade or store-bought)
¼   cup plus 1 tablespoon sugar
2   Golden Delicious apples
1   tablespoon butter
¼   pound mild blue cheese (such as Blue d'Auvergne), crumbled

Preheat oven to 350°F. Roll out dough ¼-inch thick (or to desired thickness) and cut into desired shapes. Prick crusts with a fork. Put crusts on a baking sheet and bake until golden brown. Cool on a wire rack.

Put ¼ cup of sugar on a small plate. Cut apples in half and core and stem (do not peel). Dip cut side of apple halves in sugar, then place cut-side-down on a cutting board. Slice apples, from top to bottom, into ¼-inch-thick slices, keeping slices together.

Melt butter in a skillet over medium heat. Carefully add sliced apple halves, sugared-side-down. Press lightly to cause slices to lean over against each other, but keep each group together. Sprinkle remaining 1 tablespoon of sugar over tops of apples. After about 5 minutes, raise heat to medium-high and begin to evaporate juices (the goal is to brown the bottom of the apples without burning them). The slices will slowly change color and then suddenly begin to sizzle. Remove pan from heat and check for doneness (the top of the slices should still have just a bit of crunch, with the bottoms nicely caramelized). Put 1 apple half on each baked crust, fanning the slices to expose a bit of the cooked apple between the skins. Sprinkle a little blue cheese over each apple. Serve warm.

Inn at Riverbend

The Inn at Riverbend is set on over 13 acres overlooking the New River. In summer, enjoy golfing, whitewater rafting on the New River and hiking on the Appalachian Trail. Fall in Giles County is a season you won't want to miss! The colors are vivid, the skies clear and crisp and the smell of wood smoke fills the air. Horseback riding, craft shows and Octoberfest are just a few of the delightful things to do.

Located 60 minutes west of the Roanoke airport, the inn features three-course breakfasts, free wireless internet and an evening social hour.

INNKEEPERS:	Linda & Lynn Hayes
ADDRESS:	125 River Ridge Drive
	Pearisburg, Virginia 24134
TELEPHONE:	(540) 921-5211
E-MAIL:	stay@innatriverbend.com
WEBSITE:	www.innatriverbend.com
ROOMS:	7 Rooms; Private baths
CHILDREN:	Children age 13 and older welcome
ANIMALS:	Not allowed; Resident dog
HANDICAPPED:	Handicapped accessible
DIETARY NEEDS:	Will accommodate guests' special dietary needs

Baked Brie en Croûte

Makes 4 Servings

1   sheet Pepperidge Farm puff pasty
1   (14-ounce) round Brie cheese (5-inches in diameter)
Peach chutney; strawberry preserves and chopped walnuts; or apricot
    preserves and sliced almonds, for filling
1   egg, beaten
Crackers, such as Carr's water crackers, for serving

Preheat oven to 350°F. Thaw puff pastry until soft and pliable. Roll out
puff pastry ⅛-inch thick. Trim white outer wrappings from Brie. Place Brie
in center of puff pastry. Cut a circle in puff pastry that is at least 3 times
the diameter of the brie (for a 5-inch round Brie, cut out a 15-inch round
of pastry).

Slice Brie in half and spread filling of choice over bottom half. Replace top
of Brie. Wrap puff pastry over Brie and crimp edges, sealing completely.
Brush top and sides of pastry with beaten egg. Bake for 15-20 minutes,
until hot in center and lightly browned on top. Let stand for 15 minutes.
Serve on a plate surrounded with crackers.

Old Waterstreet Inn

The Old Waterstreet Inn is a grand Federal-style brick home located in the historic district of Winchester, a lovely, small city with a historic center. Architectural details such as high ceilings, classic archways and moldings, fireplaces and a lovely staircase enhance the elegance of the inn. Just two blocks from the inn, you will find the charming walking mall with its shops, restaurants, galleries and nightlife.

The innkeepers have decorated the inn in an eclectic mix of old and new styles, creating a charming and casual ambience.

INNKEEPERS:	Jeanne Faith & Eric Erdal
ADDRESS:	217 West Boscawen Street
	Winchester, Virginia 22601
TELEPHONE:	(540) 665-6777; (866) 667-6770
E-MAIL:	oldwaterstreetinn@aol.com
WEBSITE:	www.oldwaterstreetinn.com
ROOMS:	4 Rooms; 1 Suite; Private baths
CHILDREN:	Children age 13 and older welcome
ANIMALS:	Not allowed
HANDICAPPED:	Not handicapped accessible
DIETARY NEEDS:	Will accommodate guests' special dietary needs

Zucchini & Squash Bruschetta

Makes About 15 to 20 Pieces

"This recipe is adapted from one in Gourmet *magazine. It is a big hit at our happy hour. The topping can be made ahead of time and put on the bread at the last minute." ~ Innkeeper, Old Waterstreet Inn*

1   tablespoon olive oil
1   small red onion, halved and thinly sliced
1   medium zucchini, halved and sliced ¼-inch thick
1   medium yellow squash, halved and sliced ¼-inch thick
2   cloves garlic, minced
4   Roma tomatoes, diced
½   teaspoon thyme
½   teaspoon oregano
¼   cup dry white wine (optional)
Salt and black pepper, to taste
Thin slices Provolone or Jarlsberg cheese (1 slice per slice of bread)
1   French baguette, sliced ½-inch thick

Preheat oven to 450°F. Heat oil in a skillet over medium heat. Add onion and cook until soft. Add zucchini, squash and garlic; cook until zucchini and squash are tender. Add tomatoes, thyme, oregano and white wine; cook for about 2 minutes. Season with salt and pepper; cook for about 5 minutes, until liquid is reduced by about half. Remove from heat and cool.

Put bread on a baking sheet and toast for about 4 minutes, until lightly browned. Top each slice of bread with some zucchini mixture and a slice of cheese. Bake just until cheese melts. Serve hot.

The Inn at Warner Hall

Come experience the romance and history of the Inn at Warner Hall on the plantation created in 1642 by George Washington's great-great grandfather. This wonderfully restored mansion is one of the finest country inns on the East Coast. Come savor the peace and pleasures of country life and fine dining.

"Your warm hospitality, the beauty of the décor and the excellent food were appreciated and very much enjoyed. Thanks again for a memorable experience." ~ Guest, The Inn at Warner Hall

INNKEEPERS:	Theresa & Troy Stavens
ADDRESS:	4750 Warner Hall Road
	Gloucester, Virginia 23061
TELEPHONE:	(804) 695-9565; (800) 331-2720
E-MAIL:	whall@inna.net
WEBSITE:	www.warnerhall.com
ROOMS:	9 Rooms; 2 Suites; Private baths
CHILDREN:	Children age 8 and older welcome
ANIMALS:	Not allowed; Resident dog
HANDICAPPED:	Handicapped accessible
DIETARY NEEDS:	Will accommodate guests' special dietary needs

Crab & Avocado Timbale

Makes 8 Servings

Crab:
1   tablespoon olive oil
¼   medium red onion, diced
¼   red bell pepper, diced
¼   cup mayonnaise
Lemon juice, to taste
1   tablespoon Dijon mustard
8   ounces cooked lump crabmeat

Avocado mixture:
1   avocado, diced
2   tablespoon lemon mosto olive oil, or other flavored olive oil
Juice of 1 lemon
1   ounce caviar, your favorite (optional)
¼   cup extra-virgin olive oil
16   chive spears, for garnish

For the crab: Heat olive oil in a skillet over medium-low heat. Add onion and bell pepper; cook until soft, then cool completely in refrigerator. In a bowl, combine mayonnaise, lemon juice, mustard and onion mixture. Gently fold in crabmeat. Season with salt and pepper. (Note: the crab mixture can be made up to 6 hours ahead and refrigerated).

For the avocado mixture: No more than 30 minutes before serving, combine avocado, olive oil and lemon juice (it's okay if the avocado gets mashed up a bit). Season with salt and pepper. Cover with plastic wrap, with wrap close to avocado mixture to keep out as much air as possible.

To finish: Use 8 ring molds or a clean 1¼-inch diameter plastic pvc pipe cut into 8 (2-inch) lengths. Place a mold in center of each plate. Put a little avocado mixture in each mold. Top with crabmeat and push mixture down with a small dial (or something similar). Leave mixture in mold until ready to serve. When ready to serve, using the dial, gently push down on mixture in mold while pulling mold up. Top with a small spoonful of caviar. Drizzle with extra virgin olive oil and garnish with 2 chive spears.

Bay View Waterfront

Built in the "big house/little house" style unique to the Eastern Shore, the three original sections of the circa 1800 Bay View Waterfront feature heart-pine floors, bird's-eye maple balusters, high ceilings and four fireplaces. Additions continued the Eastern Shore-style architecture until the house stretched to over 100 feet and five roof levels.

There is a large screened porch overlooking the water, where guests can enjoy the broad expanse of the creek with its variety of boats, spectacular sunsets and many waterfowl.

INNKEEPERS:	Wayne & Mary Will Browning
ADDRESS:	35350 Copes Drive
	Belle Haven, Virginia 23306
TELEPHONE:	(757) 442-6963; (800) 442-6966
E-MAIL:	browning@esva.net
WEBSITE:	www.bbhost.com/bvwaterfront
ROOMS:	1 Room; 1 Suite; Private baths
CHILDREN:	Welcome
ANIMALS:	Not allowed; Resident dogs
HANDICAPPED:	Not handicapped accessible
DIETARY NEEDS:	Will accommodate guests' special dietary needs

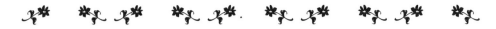

Baked Oysters

Makes 6 Servings

2   sticks butter, melted
2   sleeves Ritz crackers, crumbled into large chunks or crumbs
1   tablespoon Worcestershire sauce
1   quart fresh oysters
½   cup cream
Salt and black pepper, to taste

Preheat oven to 350°F. Grease a 9x9-inch baking dish. In a bowl, combine butter, crackers and Worcestershire; stir to combine and set aside. Heat oysters in a skillet over low heat just until slightly curled. Slowly add cream. Season with salt and pepper. Spread ½ of cracker mixture in baking dish. Top with oyster mixture, then with remaining cracker mixture. Bake for 30 minutes and serve hot.

Woodruff Inns

The chef-owned, AAA Three Diamond and Mobil Three Star Victorian Inn and Woodruff House offer unmatched European ambiance. The inns offers a truly romantic, pampered experience, nestled between the Blue Ridge Mountains in the beautiful Shenandoah Valley of Virginia.

Perfect, quiet Victorian elegance is manifest in the exclusively designed suites, cozy candlelit parlors, stained-glass dining rooms and excellently appointed drawing rooms.

INNKEEPERS:	Lucas & Deborah Woodruff
ADDRESS:	138 East Main Street
	Luray, Virginia 22835
TELEPHONE:	(540) 743-1494
E-MAIL:	woodruffinns@woodruffinns.com
WEBSITE:	www.woodruffinns.com
ROOMS:	5 Rooms; 4 Suites; 2 Cottages; Private baths
CHILDREN:	Children age 12 and older welcome
ANIMALS:	Not allowed; Resident dogs
HANDICAPPED:	Not handicapped accessible
DIETARY NEEDS:	Will accommodate guests' special dietary needs

Hot Crab Dip

Makes 4 Servings

2 (8-ounce) packages cream cheese, softened
1 cup sour cream
¼ cup blue cheese dressing
2 tablespoons key lime juice (or lime juice)
Pinch of garlic salt
2½ teaspoons Worcestershire sauce
1 teaspoon dry mustard
2 tablespoons milk
¼ cup chopped fresh dill
½ cup grated cheddar cheese
2 pounds lump crabmeat
Bread crumbs seasoned with Old Bay seasoning

Preheat oven to 400°F. Mix cream cheese, sour cream, blue cheese dressing, key lime juice, garlic salt, Worcestershire and mustard until smooth. Stir in milk and dill. Fold in cheddar cheese and crabmeat. Divide mixture among 4 (10-ounce) ramekins or other oven-proof dishes. Top with seasoned bread crumbs and bake for 10-15 minutes.

Fox Hill

Tucked into the foothills of the Blue Ridge Mountains, Fox Hill is the perfect base to explore the delights of the Shenandoah Valley. The inn is conveniently located near the Virginia Horse Center and the historic town of Lexington.

Come unwind and delight in the comfortable elegance of this 38-acre country retreat. The grounds provide endless opportunities to commune with nature – wander the lovely gardens, stroll along the spring-fed stream as the bluebirds swoop by or feed the koi in the two-tier garden pond.

INNKEEPERS:	Sue & Mark Erwin
ADDRESS:	4383 Borden Grant Trail
	Fairfield, Virginia 24435
TELEPHONE:	(540) 377-9922; (800) 369-8005
E-MAIL:	stay@foxhillbb.com
WEBSITE:	www.foxhillbb.com
ROOMS:	1 Room; 2 Suites; 2 Cottages; Private baths
CHILDREN:	Welcome
ANIMALS:	Dogs & horses welcome: Resident dog & cat
HANDICAPPED:	Not handicapped accessible
DIETARY NEEDS:	Will accommodate guests' special dietary needs

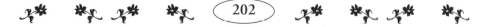

Spicy Mustard Dip

Makes 1¼ Cups

"The origin of this recipe is unknown. When we first started serving "munchies" to our guests, a friend gave me this recipe. She received it from a friend of a friend of a friend — one of those great recipes that just keeps being passed along. Serve the dip with pretzels, egg rolls, crackers or sharp cheddar cheese. It is also great as a sandwich spread." ~ Innkeeper, Fox Hill Bed & Breakfast

3   eggs
⅔   cup Coleman's dry mustard
1   cup sugar
⅔   cup cider vinegar

Whisk together all ingredients in the top of a double boiler over medium-low heat for 7-10 minutes, until thickened. Strain through a colander to remove egg white strands and serve.

York River Inn

The York River Inn Bed & Breakfast is a delightful place to enjoy the historic areas of Yorktown and Williamsburg and is the only waterfront B&B in the area. The local area is filled with historic, cultural and entertainment activities without the stress of a busy, crowded town.

Gracious settings, generous amenities and a knowledgeable host creates a memorable experience rather than just a night away from home. Breakfast is served in the elegant, antique-filled dining area overlooking the river.

INNKEEPERS: Bill Cole
ADDRESS: 209 Ambler Street
                Yorktown, Virginia 23690
TELEPHONE: (757) 887-8800; (800) 884-7003
E-MAIL: info@yorkriverinn.com
WEBSITE: www.yorkriverinn.com
ROOMS: 3 Rooms; Private baths
CHILDREN: Children age 18 and older welcome
ANIMALS: Not allowed
HANDICAPPED: Not handicapped accessible
DIETARY NEEDS: Will accommodate guests' special dietary needs

Ginger-Glazed Almonds

Makes 2 Cups

2	tablespoons butter
3	tablespoons brown sugar
2	tablespoons water
1	tablespoon finely grated fresh ginger
¼	teaspoon ground ginger
¼	teaspoon cayenne pepper
2	cups raw almonds with skins
1¼	teaspoons kosher salt

Preheat oven to 300°F. Melt butter in a small saucepan over medium-low heat. Stir in brown sugar, water, grated ginger, ground ginger and cayenne. Cook until sugar is dissolved and mixture is bubbling heavily. Add almonds and stir to coat well with butter mixture. Remove pan from heat. Add salt and stir to coat almonds.

Spread almonds in a single layer on a baking sheet. Bake for 20-25 minutes, stirring and separating frequently. Remove from oven. Cool slightly, then pour almonds onto paper towels to drain excess oil. Serve in a small bowl.

The Joshua Wilton House

O ne of Virginia's finest inns and restaurants, the Joshua Wilton House occupies a corner in the historic "Old Town" district of Harrisonburg, the heart of the beautiful and historic Shenandoah Valley. The Joshua Wilton House features five elegant rooms furnished with restored period antiques and reproductions.

The inn's award-winning restaurant features daily menus created by chef Mark Newsome. The restaurant offers a unique and exquisite seasonal menu that changes a bit each day.

INNKEEPERS:	Mark Newsome, Ann Marie Coe & Sean Pugh
ADDRESS:	412 South Main Street
	Harrisonburg, Virginia 22801
TELEPHONE:	(540) 434-4464; (888) 294-5866
E-MAIL:	info@joshuawilton.com
WEBSITE:	www.joshuawilton.com
ROOMS:	5 Rooms; Private baths
CHILDREN:	Children age 12 and older welcome
ANIMALS:	Not allowed
HANDICAPPED:	Not handicapped accessible
DIETARY NEEDS:	Will accommodate guests' special dietary needs

Spring Asparagus Salad

Makes 4 Servings

Large handful mesclun greens (mixed gourmet salad greens)*
8   ounces fresh asparagus, blanched
1   large beet, cooked, peeled and cut into batons or matchsticks
3   hard-boiled eggs, peeled and sliced
1   tablespoon toasted sesame seeds

Dressing:
½   teaspoon grated fresh ginger
½   teaspoon minced garlic
1½ teaspoons yellow miso paste*
1½ teaspoons honey
¼   cup soy sauce
¼   cup orange juice
¼   cup rice wine vinegar*
¾   cup grapeseed oil*

Layer each salad plate with greens. Arrange asparagus and beets on top of greens in center of plate. Ring with sliced egg. Sprinkle with sesame seeds and top with dressing.

For the dressing: Combine all ingredients, except grapeseed oil. While whisking, drizzle in oil until combined.

*Note: Mesclun greens, miso paste, rice wine vinegar and grapeseed oil are available at many larger grocery stores and most natural food stores.

Greenock House Inn

The Greenock House Inn is a beautiful Victorian farmhouse dating from the mid- to late-1800s. When you stay at the inn, you will be visiting over a century of history and growth.

Throughout the year, there is an everchanging profusion of blooms and foliage. Bird lovers will find binoculars and a wide variety of feathered friends from hummingbirds to yellow-bellied sapsuckers and blue birds. There is also wildlife, from groundhogs, foxes and the occasional wild turkey to the "wild" cats that patrol the grounds.

INNKEEPERS:	Lill & Rich Shearer and Andria & Brett Conyers
ADDRESS:	249 Caroline Street
	Orange, Virginia 22960
TELEPHONE:	(540) 672-3625; (800) 841-1253
E-MAIL:	availability@greenockhouse.com
WEBSITE:	www.greenockhouse.com
ROOMS:	5 Rooms; 1 Suite; 1 Cottage; Private baths
CHILDREN:	Not allowed
ANIMALS:	Not allowed
HANDICAPPED:	Not handicapped accessible
DIETARY NEEDS:	Will accommodate guests' special dietary needs

Peach & Pecan Salad with Raspberry Dressing

Makes 2 Servings

"Use different fruits and nuts in this salad to personalize it to your taste. This is our Southern version." ~ Innkeeper, Greenock House Inn

1   tablespoon butter
½   cup pecan pieces
3   cups fresh baby spinach (use a variety of greens, if desired)
2   tablespoons thinly sliced red onion
1   fresh peach, washed and cut into ½-inch cubes

Raspberry dressing:
¼   cup sugar
2   tablespoons sesame seeds
1   tablespoon poppy seeds
1½ teaspoons minced onion
¼   teaspoon Worcestershire sauce
¼   teaspoon paprika
½   cup mild olive oil
½   cup raspberry vinegar
Fresh or frozen raspberries (optional)

Melt butter in a skillet over medium-low heat. Add pecans and cook until fragrant and toasted. Toss spinach with red onion, peaches and toasted pecans. Drizzle with raspberry dressing and serve.

For the raspberry dressing: Blend all dressing ingredients, except raspberries, in a blender. Add raspberries for an extra burst of flavor, if desired.

The Shadows

Come relax in a peaceful country Victorian setting, just three miles from Montpelier. This antique-filled, stone house, built in 1913 sits on 44 acres, with gardens, gazebo, swings and old barns. Your hosts are transplanted New Yorkers who have lived in Virginia for 18 years. They have truly come to epitomize all that the phrase "Southern hospitality" means with just a bit of a New York twist.

The Peach Room features a king-size, antique burled walnut bed piled with pillows and country quilts and a unique, matching triple armoire.

INNKEEPERS:	Barbara & Pat Loffredo
ADDRESS:	14291 Constitution Highway (Route 21)
	Orange, Virginia 22960
TELEPHONE:	(540) 672-5057; (866) 672-1916
E-MAIL:	info@theshadowsbedandbreakfast.com
WEBSITE:	www.theshadowsbedandbreakfast.com
ROOMS:	4 Rooms; 1 Cottage; Private baths
CHILDREN:	Children age 10 and older welcome
ANIMALS:	Not allowed; Resident cat
HANDICAPPED:	Not handicapped accessible
DIETARY NEEDS:	Will accommodate guests' special dietary needs

Cucumber Dill Soup

Makes 4 to 6 Servings

"This soup is very refreshing on a hot summer afternoon. It is easy, but elegant, especially if beautifully presented. I like to serve it in unique cups or bowls." ~ Innkeeper, The Shadows Bed & Breakfast

4   large cucumbers, peeled, seeded and chopped
1   (8-ounce) carton sour cream
2   (10½-ounce) cans chicken broth
½   teaspoon salt
2   tablespoons chopped fresh dill plus dill sprigs, for garnish
Nasturtium flowers and leaves, for garnish (optional)

Purée cucumbers in a food processor. Add sour cream, broth, salt and chopped dill; mix well. Chill soup thoroughly. Serve garnished with a sprig of fresh dill and a nasturtium flower and leaf.

The Joshua Wilton House

The Joshua Wilton House is a brick structure with 16-inch-thick walls, built in 1888 by Joshua Wilton, a Canadian banker who moved to Harrisonburg shortly after the Civil War. After coming to Harrisonburg, he opened a foundry and a hardware store. Mr. Wilton became a prominent citizen and was responsible for bringing electricity to the area.

"The owners makes the terrific salads, breads and desserts, including a luscious crème brûlée so ethereal it could steal a Frenchman's allegiance." ~ *Bon Appetit*

INNKEEPERS:	Mark Newsome, Ann Marie Coe & Sean Pugh
ADDRESS:	412 South Main Street
	Harrisonburg, Virginia 22801
TELEPHONE:	(540) 434-4464; (888) 294-5866
E-MAIL:	info@joshuawilton.com
WEBSITE:	www.joshuawilton.com
ROOMS:	5 Rooms; Private baths
CHILDREN:	Children age 12 and older welcome
ANIMALS:	Not allowed
HANDICAPPED:	Not handicapped accessible
DIETARY NEEDS:	Will accommodate guests' special dietary needs

Sweet Potato Coconut Bisque

Makes 6 to 8 Servings

1½ teaspoons sesame oil*
1   pound sweet potatoes, peeled and diced
½   Vidalia onion (or other sweet onion), chopped
½   carrot, peeled and chopped
1½ teaspoons Thai red curry paste*
1   tablespoon palm sugar or dark brown sugar*
1   cup orange juice
2   (16-ounce) cans coconut milk*
Juice of ½ lime
Salt and black pepper, to taste

Heat oil in a soup pot over medium heat. Add sweet potatoes, onion, carrot, curry paste and palm sugar; cook for 5 minutes, until onion is translucent. Add orange juice and cook for 5 minutes. Add coconut milk and bring to a boil. Lower heat and simmer for 30 minutes. Purée with a hand blender or in batches in a food processor or blender. Stir in lime juice. Season with salt and pepper and serve.

*Note: Sesame oil, curry paste, palm sugar and coconut milk are available at many larger grocery stores and most natural food stores (such as Whole Foods or Wild Oats).

Luncheon & Dinner Entrées

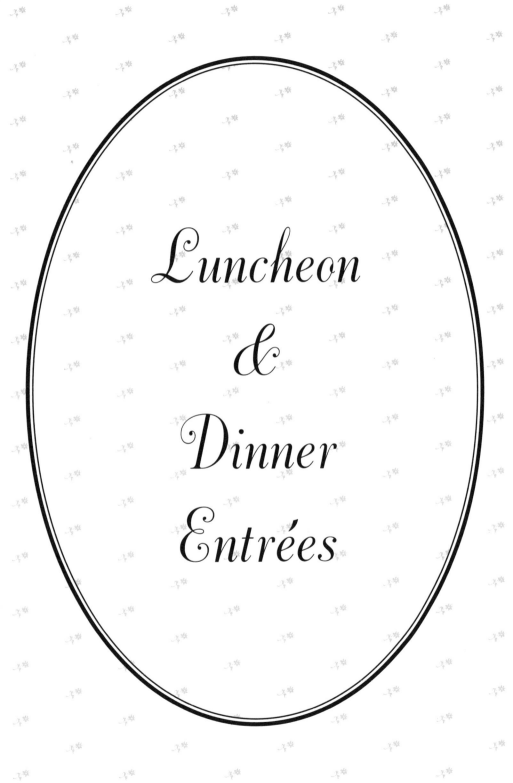

Luncheon
&
Dinner
Entrées

Inn at Court Square

S ituated two blocks from the historic downtown pedestrian mall, one mile from the University of Virginia and four miles from Monticello and Ashlawn, the Inn at Court Square provides pampering in a peaceful neighborhood, conveniently located near Charlottesville's many historic sites and arts and entertainment venues.

The inn's lavish continental breakfasts highlight the delicious creations of Pastry Chef Pat Chiavetta. Guests rave about Chef Karl Bock's exquisite luncheons featuring homemade soups, salads and gourmet sandwiches.

INNKEEPERS:	Candace DeLoach
ADDRESS:	410 East Jefferson Street
	Charlottesville, Virginia 22902
TELEPHONE:	(434) 295-2800; (866) 466-2877
E-MAIL:	innatcourtsquare@aol.com
WEBSITE:	www.innatcourtsquare.com
ROOMS:	7 Rooms; Private baths
CHILDREN:	Children age 12 and older welcome
ANIMALS:	Not allowed
HANDICAPPED:	Not handicapped accessible
DIETARY NEEDS:	Will accommodate guests' special dietary needs

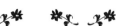

Lime Chipotle Chicken Salad

Makes 4 to 6 Servings

"This is one of my favorites. It serves four as a sandwich filling and six as a salad with greens. I use a spring mix with Roma tomatoes and a sun-dried tomato vinaigrette at the inn for lunch." ~ Chef Karl Bock, The Inn at Court Square

2	pounds boneless, skinless chicken breast
1	tablespoon chipotle pepper powder*
2	tablespoons cumin
2	teaspoons kosher salt
1	teaspoon freshly ground black pepper
3	limes
3	tablespoons olive oil
½	cup water
3	tablespoons mayonnaise
1	bunch green onions, thinly sliced
¼	cup chopped fresh cilantro

Rinse chicken and trim any excess fat. Put chicken in a bowl. Combine chipotle powder, cumin, salt and pepper; add to chicken and toss to coat. Let stand for 10-15 minutes. Juice 2 limes and pour over chicken; toss chicken to coat and let stand for 10 minutes more.

Heat oil in a large skillet over medium-high heat. Cook chicken in batches until done; remove to a platter and cool. Drain excess oil from skillet. Add water to skillet and deglaze skillet, reducing liquid to about ¼ cup. Juice remaining lime and add to liquid in skillet; cool.

When chicken is cool to the touch, shred it with your fingers into a bowl. Add liquid from skillet and toss chicken to coat. Mix in mayonnaise. Mix in green onions and cilantro. Adjust seasonings, if needed, and serve.

*Note: Chipotle powder is made from dried, smoked red jalapeño peppers. It is smoky, spicy and very rich in flavor. It is available at some gourmet and grocery stores or from Penzeys Spices (www.penzeys.com).

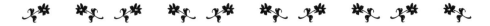

The Shadows

B reakfast at the Shadows Bed & Breakfast Inn is served in the Hunt Dining Room, named for the one-of-a-kind Civil War-era sideboard that commands the room. The menu changes daily, so plan to stay long enough to be treated to such specialties as stuffed French toast or other mouth-watering specialties, presented on fine china and crystal.

The Blue Room is an elegant and serene bedroom distinguished by its queen-sized walnut bed from the Civil War period. A daybed, piled high with lace pillows provides extra sleeping accommodations.

INNKEEPERS:	Barbara & Pat Loffredo
ADDRESS:	14291 Constitution Highway (Route 21)
	Orange, Virginia 22960
TELEPHONE:	(540) 672-5057; (866) 672-1916
E-MAIL:	info@theshadowsbedandbreakfast.com
WEBSITE:	www.theshadowsbedandbreakfast.com
ROOMS:	4 Rooms; 1 Cottage; Private baths
CHILDREN:	Children age 10 and older welcome
ANIMALS:	Not allowed; Resident cat
HANDICAPPED:	Not handicapped accessible
DIETARY NEEDS:	Will accommodate guests' special dietary needs

Monte Cristo

Makes 4 Servings

"This is about as elegant as a hearty sandwich can get – it makes a great light meal." ~ Innkeeper, The Shadows Bed & Breakfast

¼ cup Dijon mustard
8 slices sourdough bread
½ pound sliced Virginia ham
½ pound sliced smoked turkey breast
¼ pound sliced Swiss or havarti cheese
1 (12-ounce) jar roasted sweet red peppers
8 eggs
1 stick butter, divided
Powdered sugar

Spread mustard over 4 slices of bread. Top with ham, turkey, cheese and red peppers. Top with remaining bread. Beat eggs in a shallow dish or plate. Melt ½ stick of butter in a skillet over medium heat. Dip each sandwich in beaten egg, turning to coat. Add 2 sandwiches to skillet and cook until browned on each side. Repeat with remaining butter and sandwiches. Sprinkle each sandwich with powdered sugar. Dress up with a few sweet pickle slices and serve.

High Meadows Vineyard Inn

E scape from the ordinary and fall in love with romantic High Meadows Vineyard Inn, a Virginia Historic Landmark, listed on the National Register. In 1832, 100 years after the settlement of Scottsville, surveyor Peter White built the Federalist portion of the inn. Businessman Charles Harris constructed the Victorian portion of the inn in 1882.

The restaurant at High Meadows is an elegant dining experience in a casual setting. It is a "Virginia Wine Restaurant of the Year" and a distinguished member of *Gourmet Magazine's* "2002 Restaurant Hall of Fame."

INNKEEPERS:	Rose Farber & Jon Storey
ADDRESS:	55 High Meadows Lane
	Scottsville, Virginia 24590
TELEPHONE:	(434) 286-2218; (800) 232-1832
E-MAIL:	highmeadows@earthlink.net
WEBSITE:	www.highmeadows.com
ROOMS:	12 Rooms; 3 Suites; 3 Cottages; Private baths
CHILDREN:	Welcome
ANIMALS:	Not allowed; Resident dog
HANDICAPPED:	Not handicapped accessible
DIETARY NEEDS:	Will accommodate guests' special dietary needs

Asian Pork Tenderloin with Garlic Mirin Reduction

Makes 4 Servings

"A sweet and spicy pork tenderloin. It is best if the meat marinates overnight."
~ Innkeeper, High Meadows Vineyard Inn

2	pork tenderloins (about 1½-2 pounds total), trimmed
½	cup soy sauce
1¼	cups honey
1¼	cups mirin*
2	tablespoons minced garlic
2	tablespoons red pepper flakes

Put pork in a casserole dish. Whisk together soy sauce, honey, mirin, garlic and red pepper flakes; pour over pork. Cover and refrigerate overnight, turning once.

The next day, preheat oven to 350°F. Remove pork from marinade (reserve marinade) and bake for 20-30 minutes, until a meat thermometer inserted in center of pork registers 150°F. Tent with foil and let stand for 10 minutes.

While pork is roasting, strain marinade and pour into a saucepan. Bring to a boil, lower heat and simmer until sauce thickens, about 30 minutes. Serve sauce over sliced pork.

*Note: Mirin is a sweet Japanese cooking wine, also known as rice wine. It is available in the Asian section of most grocery stores.

White Birches Inn

W hite Birches Inn is an early 20th-century, English Country-style home located in Abingdon's historic district. This finely preserved home has been totally updated and renovated both inside and out. Guest rooms are named in honor of famous playwrights who bartered their plays for Virginia ham at Abingdon's world-famous Barter Theatre.

Rooms are furnished with all the amenities discriminating guests require – plush velour robes, Egyptian cotton towels, high-end linens and thick, billowy comforters.

INNKEEPERS:	Michael & Paulette Wartella
ADDRESS:	268 Whitesmill Road
	Abingdon, Virginia 24210
TELEPHONE:	(276) 676-2140; (800) 247-2437
E-MAIL:	stay@whitebirchesinn.com
WEBSITE:	www.whitebirchesinn.com
ROOMS:	2 Rooms; 3 Suites; Private baths
CHILDREN:	Children age 12 and older welcome
ANIMALS:	Not allowed; Resident dog
HANDICAPPED:	Call ahead
DIETARY NEEDS:	Will accommodate guests' special dietary needs

Linguini with Sausage & Spinach

Makes 6 Servings

"A quick and easy one-pot meal – as the ingredients are cooking, the sauce is formed." - Innkeeper, White Birches Inn

3	tablespoons olive oil
1	pound hot or mild link sausage, cut into bite-size pieces
1	large Vidalia onion (or other sweet onion), chopped
2	cloves garlic, chopped
4	cups chicken broth
½	cup water
1	pound linguini, broken in half
2	(9-ounce) packages frozen (thawed) chopped spinach
1	teaspoon black pepper
½	cup heavy cream

Heat oil in a 5-quart Dutch oven over medium heat. Add sausage and cook until done. Add onions and garlic; cook until browned. Raise heat to high, add broth and water, cover and bring to boil. Lower heat to medium-high, add pasta and cook for 4 minutes, stirring frequently. Add spinach and pepper; cook for 2 minutes more, or until pasta is al dente. Remove from heat, stir in heavy cream and serve.

Crump's Mountain Cottage

C rump's Mountain Cottage offers a two-bedroom cabin with panoramic views of the mountains and valley below from the deck. Enjoy the soothing sounds of the mountain stream cascading past the cottage. Marvel at the star-studded night sky. Explore 116 wooded acres – the area is ideal for hikers, mountain bikers, nature lovers and anyone seeking solitude. In fall, see how apple butter and cider are made on the innkeepers' orchard.

Within an hour are the Blue Ridge Parkway, Appomattox Historic Park (where Lee surrendered to Grant), Monticello and the Appalachian Trail.

INNKEEPERS:	Carolyn & Curtis Crump
ADDRESS:	2150 Indian Creek Road
	Amherst, Virginia 24521
TELEPHONE:	(434) 277-5563; (866) 868-4118
E-MAIL:	crumpmtcottage@pngusa.net
WEBSITE:	www.bbonline.com/va/crumps
ROOMS:	1 Cottage; Private bath
CHILDREN:	Welcome
ANIMALS:	Dogs & cats welcome
HANDICAPPED:	Not handicapped accessible
DIETARY NEEDS:	Will accommodate guests' special dietary needs

Kielbase & Potatoes

Makes 6 Servings

"This recipe was taught to me by my mother, who learned it from her mother, who immigrated to the United States from Hungary." ~ Innkeeper, Crump's Mountain Cottage

3-4 strips bacon, quartered
1   large onion, chopped
1-2 tablespoons Hungarian paprika
½   cup water plus more as needed
1   pound kielbase, halved and cut into ¼-inch-thick slices
5   large white potatoes
Salt and black pepper, to taste

Cook bacon in a 3-quart saucepan over medium heat until most of fat is rendered. Add onion and cook until almost translucent. Stir in paprika. Add ½ cup of water, kielbase and potatoes. Add enough water to come ½-inch beneath top of ingredients in saucepan. Season with salt and pepper. Cover pan and bring to a boil. Lower heat and simmer for 25 minutes, or until potatoes are tender.

Old Spring Farm

Whatever the season, whatever the reason, Old Spring Farm Bed & Breakfast is a quintessential mountain getaway located 50 miles south of Roanoke on the Blue Ridge Parkway. Built in 1883, with money made from selling moonshine, Old Spring Farm Bed & Breakfast is today a working farm located in Blue Ridge wine country.

Eggs produced on the inn's farm are used in a variety of casseroles, omelets and quiches. Expect a hearty gourmet breakfast beginning with fresh breads with homemade jellies made from ten varieties of farm-raised fruit.

INNKEEPERS:	Suzanne V. Pabst
ADDRESS:	7629 Charity Highway
	Woolwine, Virginia 24185
TELEPHONE:	(276) 930-3404
E-MAIL:	Not available
WEBSITE:	www.oldspringfarm.com
ROOMS:	6 Rooms; Private & shared baths
CHILDREN:	Children age 6 and older welcome
ANIMALS:	Not allowed; Resident dog & cat
HANDICAPPED:	Call ahead
DIETARY NEEDS:	Will accommodate guests' special dietary needs

Rosemary Lamb Chops

Makes 4 Servings

"If ever there was a signature dish at Old Spring Farm, this is it! Farm-raised Barbados lamb and these few ingredients keep guests coming back for more. This recipe is good for any cut of lamb. Plan ahead, the lamb needs to marinate for at least one day." ~ Innkeeper, Old Spring Farm Bed & Breakfast

¼   cup olive oil
¼   cup balsamic vinegar
2   tablespoons chopped fresh rosemary (or 2 teaspoons dried)
2   tablespoons fresh lime juice
¼   teaspoon coarsely ground black pepper or Montreal steak seasoning
½   teaspoon kosher salt, or more to taste
4   cloves garlic, chopped, or more to taste
4   green onions, sliced
8   lamb loin or rib chops

Combine all ingredients, except lamb, in a large zipper plastic bag. Add lamb and turn to coat. Seal bag and refrigerate overnight, turning occasionally.

The next day, about 45 minutes prior to cooking, let lamb come to room temperature. Preheat grill or broiler. Grill or broil lamb for 4½-5 minutes per side for medium-rare or 6 minutes per side for medium.

Woodruff Inns

E specially designed to pamper you in every way, many of the Woodruff Inns' romantic guest rooms feature fireside Jacuzzis. The two riverside cottages offer peaceful privacy and hot tubs overlooking the beautiful Shenandoah River. Upon arrival, you will enjoy a delightful candlelit "afternoon dessert tea" with cakes, cookies and pastries.

The Woodruff Inns were featured in the March, 2000 edition of *Food and Wine Magazine* as "One of Virginia's Best Restaurants."

INNKEEPERS:	Lucas & Deborah Woodruff
ADDRESS:	138 East Main Street
	Luray, Virginia 22835
TELEPHONE:	(540) 743-1494
E-MAIL:	woodruffinns@woodruffinns.com
WEBSITE:	www.woodruffinns.com
ROOMS:	5 Rooms; 4 Suites; 2 Cottages; Private baths
CHILDREN:	Children age 12 and older welcome
ANIMALS:	Not allowed; Resident dogs
HANDICAPPED:	Not handicapped accessible
DIETARY NEEDS:	Will accommodate guests' special dietary needs

Crab Cakes

Makes 8 Servings

2   slices bread, broken into small pieces
2   tablespoons milk
1   large egg, beaten
¼   teaspoon salt
1   tablespoon chopped fresh dill
1   teaspoon Old Bay seasoning
1   tablespoon baking powder
1   tablespoon Worcestershire sauce
1   tablespoon blue cheese dressing
1   pound lump crabmeat
2   tablespoons butter or vegetable oil

Put bread in a bowl and moisten with milk. Add egg, salt, dill, Old Bay seasoning, baking powder, Worcestershire and blue cheese dressing; stir to combine. Fold in crabmeat. Shape mixture into 8 small patties. Melt butter in a skillet over medium heat. Add crab cakes and cook until browned on each side.

The Inn at Narrow Passage

True colonial inns were built along the major trails and toll roads of early America. So it is with the Inn at Narrow Passage. With its oldest section built around 1740, the inn has been welcoming travelers along the Great Wagon Road (now U.S. Route 11) for almost 250 years.

The inn's sturdy log walls made it a safe haven against Indian attacks at the "narrow passage" – where the road was only one wagon wide and traveling was very dangerous. Later, it became important as Stonewall Jackson's headquarters during the Valley Campaign of 1862.

INNKEEPERS:	Ellen & Ed Markel
ADDRESS:	Route 11 South at Chapman Landing Road
	Woodstock, Virginia 22664
TELEPHONE:	(540) 459-8000; (800) 459-8002
E-MAIL:	innkeeper@innatnarrowpassage.com
WEBSITE:	www.innatnarrowpassage.com
ROOMS:	12 Rooms; Private baths
CHILDREN:	Welcome
ANIMALS:	Not allowed
HANDICAPPED:	Handicapped accessible
DIETARY NEEDS:	Will accommodate guests' special dietary needs

Hazelnut-Crusted Salmon

Makes 4 Servings

1	(16-ounce) salmon fillet
1	teaspoon salt, divided
4	tablespoons fresh lemon juice, divided
¾	stick butter, softened
1	tablespoon chopped fresh parsley
1	tablespoon chopped fresh dill
⅓	cup freshly grated Parmesan cheese
⅓	cup bread crumbs, toasted
½	cup coarsely chopped hazelnuts, roasted and skinned*

Preheat oven to 450°F. Rinse salmon in cold water and pat dry. Lightly coat a baking dish with oil or spray with non-stick cooking spray. Sprinkle salmon with ½ teaspoon of salt. Brush with 2 tablespoons of lemon juice.

In a small bowl, combine remaining 2 tablespoons of lemon juice, butter, parsley and dill; stir until smooth and well blended. Add Parmesan cheese, bread crumbs, remaining ½ teaspoon of salt and hazelnuts; stir to combine, then pat over top of salmon.

Bake salmon for 10-15 minutes, until firm. Raise oven temperature to broil. Broil salmon for about 1 minute, until top is bubbling and lightly browned.

*Note: To roast hazelnuts, spread shelled hazelnuts on a baking sheet and bake in a preheated 275°F oven for 20 minutes, stirring occasionally. Remove hazelnuts from oven and rub briskly with a towel while still warm to remove skins.

Williamsburg Sampler

The six bedrooms in the Williamsburg Sampler Bed & Breakfast Inn compliment the ones located in the historic area. The rooms serve as wonderful replicas of an elegant Colonial home with antiques, pewter and framed American and English samplers. The four bed chambers, which include suites with "roof-top gardens," are cozy, with pineapple-carved, four-poster beds, colonial décor, central air and private baths.

"The food and service are wonderful … with the standards of the best hotel." ~ Arno Schmidt, Executive Chef (retired), the Waldorf-Astoria

INNKEEPERS:	Ike Sisane
ADDRESS:	922 Jamestown Road
	Williamsburg, Virginia 23185
TELEPHONE:	(757) 253-0398; (800) 722-1169
E-MAIL:	info@williamsburgsampler.com
WEBSITE:	www.williamsburgsampler.com
ROOMS:	2 Rooms; 2 Suites; Private baths
CHILDREN:	Children age 12 and older welcome
ANIMALS:	Not allowed
HANDICAPPED:	Not handicapped accessible
DIETARY NEEDS:	Will accommodate guests' special dietary needs

Plantation Gumbo

Makes 8 to 10 Servings

1   pint fresh okra, washed
2   tablespoons lard (or vegetable oil)
2   large onions, chopped
1   large slice ham, cut into squares
6   fresh tomatoes, chopped (juice reserved)
24 fresh oysters
1   pound fresh shrimp
1   cup crabmeat
1   red chile pepper, seeded and chopped
2   bay leaves
2   sprigs parsley, chopped (leaves only)
1   sprig thyme, chopped (leaves only)
2   teaspoons gumbo file
3   quarts water
Salt and black pepper, to taste
Cooked rice, for serving

Steam okra and leave whole. Melt lard in a soup pot over medium heat. Add onions, ham and okra; cook until onions are well browned. Stir in tomatoes with juice. Add oysters, shrimp and crab. Stir in chile pepper, bay leaves, parsley, thyme and gumbo file. When everything is well cooked and browned, add water. Let simmer gently for 1 hour or longer. Season to taste with salt and pepper. Serve over rice in a bowl.

Long Hill

S ituated at the northern end of the Shenandoah Valley, Long Hill Bed & Breakfast makes an ideal destination for day trips into Washington, D.C., and to many historic sites in Virginia and surrounding states. Long Hill was named one of the top 15 B&B's in North America by *Arrington's 2003 Book of Lists* in the category of "Best Breakfast."

The Long Hill breakfast is varied throughout your stay and is served at your convenience. Breakfast may include baked fruit compote, Long Hill breakfast pie, caramel French toast, grits soufflé and country ham.

INNKEEPERS:	George & Rhoda Kriz
ADDRESS:	547 Apple Pie Ridge Road
	Winchester, Virginia 22603
TELEPHONE:	(540) 450-0341; (866) 450-0341
E-MAIL:	longhillbb@longhillbb.com
WEBSITE:	www.longhillbb.com
ROOMS:	3 Rooms; Private baths
CHILDREN:	Not allowed
ANIMALS:	Not allowed
HANDICAPPED:	Handicapped accessible
DIETARY NEEDS:	Will accommodate guests' special dietary needs

Blue Ribbon Chili

Makes About 1 Gallon

"This recipe won the Roanoke Valley recipe contest in 1974. It is a mild and delicious chili. Make it at least one or two days prior to serving to let the flavors develop. Reheat it gently so as not to scorch it, or reheat just the amount you need and refrigerate or freeze the rest." ~ Innkeeper, Long Hill Bed & Breakfast

1	pound lean ground beef, buffalo or venison
½	pound hot link sausage, sliced
½	pound mild link sausage, sliced
1	tablespoon butter or oil
1	large onion, chopped
1	medium green bell pepper, chopped
1	teaspoon salt
1½	tablespoons chili powder
½	teaspoon black pepper
1½	teaspoons cumin
¼	teaspoon allspice
2	(14-ounce) cans tomatoes
2	(14-ounce) cans kidney beans
1½	tablespoons sugar
½	square (½ ounce) semi-sweet baking chocolate
1	bay leaf
1	(6-ounce) can tomato paste
1	(12-ounce) can condensed beef consommé

Grated cheddar cheese, for serving
Sour cream, for serving

Brown ground beef and hot and mild sausage in a large, heavy Dutch oven or soup pot over medium heat; set aside in a colander to drain grease. Add butter or oil (or 1 tablespoon of grease from meat), onion and bell pepper to Dutch oven; cook until onion is translucent. Add meat and remaining ingredients, except cheese and sour cream; stir well. Bring to a boil, lower heat and simmer gently for 3 hours. Remove bay leaf. Cover and refrigerate for 24-48 hours. Reheat and serve with grated cheese and sour cream.

Fruit Specialties & Beverages

Fruit Specialties & Beverages

Inn at Tabb's Creek Landing

The Inn at Tabb's Creek Landing was originally the antebellum home of a local sea captain. Built in the 1820s on the banks of Tabb's Creek, the original house is surrounded by screened porches and reading rooms. A separate cottage contains two suites and a separate bedroom.

Just two and one-half hours from Washington and one and one-half hours from Richmond, great restaurants and day trips abound. You are within 35 minutes of Williamsburg and Yorktown, with Newport News and Norfolk just a little further away.

INNKEEPERS:	Bill & Erin Rogers
ADDRESS:	384 Turpin Lane
	Matthews-Port Haywood, Virginia 23138
TELEPHONE:	(804) 725-5136
E-MAIL:	tabbscreeklanding@hotmail.com
WEBSITE:	None available
ROOMS:	4 Rooms; 3 Suites; Private & shared baths
CHILDREN:	Welcome
ANIMALS:	Not allowed
HANDICAPPED:	Handicapped accessible
DIETARY NEEDS:	Will accommodate guests' special dietary needs

Layered Fruit Trifle

Makes 12 Servings

"This trifle is light and fruity. It's wonderful for brunch." ~ Innkeeper, Inn at Tabb's Creek Landing

1   (8-ounce) carton Cool Whip
1   (4-ounce) box instant vanilla pudding
Pound cake (see recipe on page 299 or use store-bought), cut into
    small cubes
¼   cup orange juice
Sliced fresh strawberries
Sliced fresh kiwi
1   (20-ounce) can pineapple tidbits
2   (15-ounce) cans mandarin oranges
3   large bananas, sliced

Combine Cool Whip and instant pudding; cover and chill. In a clear trifle dish, place a layer of pound cake. Sprinkle with orange juice. Top with some of the Cool Whip mixture. Top with a layer of fruit, using 1 type of fruit at a time. Repeat layers, ending with a pretty layer of fruit.

Fleeton Fields

The Fleeton Fields Bed & Breakfast is a lovely colonial-style inn nestled in a park-like setting in an area of large properties and beautiful homes. Inside the inn, fresh flowers and quiet music set the stage for a relaxing getaway. The inn features fine Victorian and period furnishings while still providing the modern amenities required by discerning travelers.

After a day of enjoying the natural and historic attractions of the Northern Neck and Tangier Island, you can choose a nearby waterfront restaurant for a delicious dinner of fresh Chesapeake Bay seafood and local specialties.

INNKEEPERS:	Marguerite Slaughter
ADDRESS:	2783 Fleeton Road
	Reedville, Virginia 22539
TELEPHONE:	(804) 453-5014; (800) 497-8215
E-MAIL:	info@fleetonfields.com
WEBSITE:	www.fleetonfields.com
ROOMS:	3 Suites; Private baths
CHILDREN:	Welcome
ANIMALS:	Welcome; Call ahead
HANDICAPPED:	Not handicapped accessible
DIETARY NEEDS:	Will accommodate guests' special dietary needs

Berry Torte

Makes 6 to 8 Servings

"A beautiful and delicious breakfast torte that will impress your guests." ~ Innkeeper, Fleeton Fields Bed & Breakfast

1	cup all-purpose flour
¼	cup plus 2 tablespoons sugar
1½	teaspoons baking powder
½	teaspoon baking soda
½	teaspoon salt
2	tablespoons butter
1	egg, separated
1	tablespoon almond extract
½	teaspoon vanilla extract
⅓	cup sour cream (or light sour cream)
½	cup milk
½	(8-ounce) package cream cheese
3	tablespoons raspberry preserves

Fresh or frozen blueberries, for topping
Craisins or dried cranberries, for topping
Slivered almonds, for topping

Preheat oven to 365°F. Spray a 9-inch round cake pan with a removable bottom with non-stick cooking spray. In a large bowl, combine flour, ¼ cup of sugar, baking powder, baking soda and salt. Cut in butter. In a medium bowl, combine egg yolk, almond and vanilla extracts, sour cream and milk; add to flour mixture and stir to combine. Pour batter into pan.

Mix egg white, cream cheese and remaining 2 tablespoons of sugar; dot on top of batter. With a fork, trail or drizzle raspberry preserves over batter. Sprinkle blueberries, Craisins and almonds over batter. Bake for about 25 minutes, until center is set.

Three Angels Inn at Sherwood

The Three Angels Inn at Historic Sherwood Plantation was built in 1883, during the tumultuous years after the Civil War. The house first served as a hospital, caring for the area's African-American population.

In this day, such an undertaking may not seem out of the ordinary, but in a time when African-Americans could not find medical attention, education or any of the necessities we take for granted, one woman, Patti Buford, answered the cry of an entire race, providing the love and attention they so desperately needed.

INNKEEPERS: Tom & Pat Krewson
ADDRESS: 236 Pleasant Grove Road
                   Lawrenceville, Virginia 23868
TELEPHONE: (434) 848-0830; (877) 777-4264
E-MAIL: innkeeper@threeangelsinn.com
WEBSITE: www.threeangelsinn.com
ROOMS: 4 Rooms; Private baths
CHILDREN: Call ahead
ANIMALS: Not allowed
HANDICAPPED: Not handicapped accessible
DIETARY NEEDS: Will accommodate guests' special dietary needs

Dark Sweet Cherry Cobbler

Makes 4 Servings

"Served in champagne glasses, topped with whipped cream and a sprinkle of freshly grated nutmeg, this is an elegant dessert that belies its ease of preparation." ~ Innkeeper, Three Angels Inn at Sherwood

1	stick butter or margarine, melted
1	cup all-purpose flour
1	cup sugar
2	teaspoons baking powder
¾	cup milk (can use skim)
¼	teaspoon salt
1	(15-ounce) can dark sweet cherries (reserve ½ of cherry juice)

Whipped cream, for garnish
Freshly grated nutmeg, for garnish

Preheat oven to 350°F. Spray an 8x8-inch baking pan with non-stick cooking spray. Combine butter, flour, sugar, baking powder, milk and salt; spread in pan. Top with cherries and drizzle with reserved cherry juice.

Bake for about 40 minutes, until top in browned. Serve in champagne glasses. Garnish with whipped cream and a sprinkle of grated nutmeg.

Note: This cobbler cannot be frozen, but it can be made earlier in the day and refrigerated.

Smithfield Farm

S mithfield Farm offers many ways to pass the time. If you seek quiet leisure, the grounds include a gazebo and water garden, creating a peaceful backdrop while you drift off in the hammock. If you wish to explore further, go for a hike on the nature trail through the old orchard. Or, stop by the farm store and take home some of the farm's all-natural beef, pork and eggs as a tasty reminder of your stay at Smithfield Farm.

Smithfield Farm is a seventh-generation family farm! Today, it is a 350-acre organic farm, specializing in free-range meats.

INNKEEPERS:	Ruth & Betsy Pritchard
ADDRESS:	568 Smithfield Lane
	Berryville, Virginia 22611
TELEPHONE:	(877) 955-4389
E-MAIL:	info@smithfieldfarm.com
WEBSITE:	www.smithfieldfarm.com
ROOMS:	3 Rooms; Private baths
CHILDREN:	Children age 12 and older welcome
ANIMALS:	Not allowed; Resident dog
HANDICAPPED:	Not handicapped accessible
DIETARY NEEDS:	Will accommodate guests' special dietary needs

Apple Brown Betsy

Makes 4 Servings

"We are a working cattle and apple farm, so we incorporate our products into what we serve our guests. Betsy has become famous for her own version of our 'fresh from the farm' desserts, which were featured in Gourmet *magazine." ~ Innkeeper, Smithfield Farm Bed & Breakfast*

4	cups chopped tart apples (peeled, if desired)
¼	cup orange juice
1	cup sugar
¾	cup sifted all-purpose flour
½	teaspoon cinnamon plus extra for garnish
¼	teaspoon nutmeg

Dash of salt

1	stick butter
¼	cup old-fashioned rolled oats
¼	cup granola

Vanilla ice cream, for serving

Preheat oven to 375°F. Grease a deep-dish pie pan or an 8x8-inch baking dish. Put apples in a large bowl and sprinkle with orange juice; toss to combine. Put apples in pie pan or baking dish.

In a medium bowl, combine sugar, flour, cinnamon, nutmeg and salt. Cut butter into sugar mixture until crumbly; sprinkle over apples. Sprinkle with oats and granola. Dust with cinnamon. Bake for 45 minutes. Serve warm with ice cream.

York River Inn

The York River Inn, set on a high bluff overlooking the York River in a Colonial-style home, is the only waterfront bed & breakfast in the Yorktown and Colonial Williamsburg area. The inn is the ideal location for a relaxing visit to historic Yorktown, and is just 15 minutes from Colonial Williamsburg by way of the scenic Colonial Parkway.

"A stay at the York River Inn B&B is not just a stay, but a total experience. The atmosphere, furnishings and hospitality are unique … but breakfast is a pure work of art." ~ Guest, York River Inn Bed & Breakfast

INNKEEPERS: Bill Cole
ADDRESS: 209 Ambler Street
                 Yorktown, Virginia 23690
TELEPHONE: (757) 887-8800; (800) 884-7003
E-MAIL: info@yorkriverinn.com
WEBSITE: www.yorkriverinn.com
ROOMS: 3 Rooms; Private baths
CHILDREN: Children age 18 and older welcome
ANIMALS: Not allowed
HANDICAPPED: Not handicapped accessible
DIETARY NEEDS: Will accommodate guests' special dietary needs

Poached Pears with Cranberries

Makes 6 Servings

3   pears, halved and cored
2   tablespoon orange marmalade
½   cup sugar
¼   teaspoon salt
2   tablespoons butter, melted
1   cup cranberries, cut in half or coarsely chopped
2   tablespoons orange juice concentrate
2   tablespoons water
6-12   tablespoons (¾ cup) sour cream

Preheat oven to 350°F. Spray a casserole dish with non-stick cooking spray. Put pears fairly close together in casserole dish, cut-side-down. Combine marmalade, sugar, salt, butter, cranberries, orange juice concentrate and water; pour over pears.

Bake pears for about 30 minutes, or until pears are tender enough to cut with a fork, but not mushy. Put 1 pear, round-side-down, in each serving bowl. Put 1-2 tablespoons of sour cream into the hole in each pear. Pour a little pan sauce over each pear and serve.

River's Edge

River's Edge is a mix of old and new, with the original section built in 1913 and the new section added in 1996. A wrap-around porch with rocking chairs, a hammock under the trees, a bench by the river, a formal flower garden and hiking paths give you places to explore or sit quietly.

The Orchard Room has wonderful views in three directions – over the river, the orchard and vegetable gardens, and the wooded hillside. It has the inn's most elegant bath, with a soaking tub and a separate shower.

INNKEEPERS:	Lee Britton
ADDRESS:	6208 Little Camp Road
	Riner, Virginia 24149
TELEPHONE:	(540) 381-4147; (888) 746-9418
E-MAIL:	innkeeper@river-edge.com
WEBSITE:	www.river-edge.com
ROOMS:	4 Rooms; Private baths
CHILDREN:	Welcome
ANIMALS:	Dogs welcome; Resident cats
HANDICAPPED:	Handicapped accessible
DIETARY NEEDS:	Will accommodate guests' special dietary needs

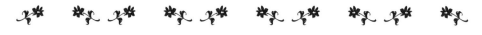

Bananas in Cream

Makes 4 to 6 Servings

"I once found a recipe called 'Bananas Tropicale' that sounded delicious and tasted awful – but it gave me ideas for this dish. Most people can guess that it contains sour cream and brown sugar, but the pineapple juice and cardamom are the surprise ingredients." ~ Innkeeper, River's Edge

1	cup low-fat sour cream
2	tablespoons packed brown sugar
2	tablespoons pineapple juice
¼	teaspoon ground cardamom
4	bananas, sliced

Combine sour cream, brown sugar, pineapple juice and cardamom; mix well. Put bananas into a serving dish and top with sour cream mixture.

Breezy Oaks Farm House

B reezy Oaks Farm House Bed & Breakfast is an 18th-century farmhouse refurbished for your comfort and enjoyment. Experience a good night's rest, fireside candle-lit dinners and therapeutic massage for individuals or couples. Wake up to an organic breakfast to begin your day.

Breezy Oaks is located just four miles from Virginia International Raceway and VIR Euro Rally, "the school and corporate motorsport experience." The inn is also an excellent base from which to tour Civil War sites in southeastern Virginia, including Danville's Lost Gold Shipment.

INNKEEPERS:	Linda Zuniga & Gray Williamson
ADDRESS:	2115 Calvary Road
	Alton, Virginia 24520
TELEPHONE:	(434) 822-5841
E-MAIL:	breezyoaks@gamewood.net
WEBSITE:	www.innvirginia.com
ROOMS:	6 Rooms; Private & shared baths
CHILDREN:	Welcome
ANIMALS:	Not allowed; Resident cats
HANDICAPPED:	Call ahead
DIETARY NEEDS:	Will accommodate guests' special dietary needs

Chilled Strawberry Soup

Makes 8 Servings

2   cups strawberries, sliced plus 8 whole strawberries, for garnish
2   (8-ounce) cartons strawberry yogurt with fruit on bottom
1   nectarine, peeled and sliced
1   peach, peeled and sliced
1   tablespoon natural cane sugar (raw sugar)
2   tablespoons fresh lemon juice
Whipped cream
8   fresh mint sprigs, for garnish
8   demi-glasses Asti Spumante or other sweet sparkling wine

Combine sliced strawberries, yogurt, nectarine, peach, sugar and lemon juice in a blender or food processor; blend until smooth. Cover and chill.

Divide strawberry mixture among serving bowls. Put a dollop of whipped cream in center of each serving. Top with a mint sprig. Slice the 8 whole strawberries almost through and fan 1 strawberry atop each serving. Serve with glasses of Asti Spumante to sip while enjoying the flavors of the soup.

The Mountain Rose Inn

B uilt at the turn of the century by Joseph H. DeHart, the house which is now the Mountain Rose Inn faced the site of the famed Mountain Rose Distillery Number 250. One of the few legal distilleries in Virginia, the Mountain Rose, known for "honest goods" and "full measure," produced such delicacies as Old Ike rye whiskey and Mountain Dew and Pride of Virginia corn whiskeys.

The quality of goods produced by the Mountain Rose was so good, it is said to have supplied the White House with spirits during Prohibition!

INNKEEPERS:	Reeves & Melodie Pogue
ADDRESS:	1787 Charity Highway
	Woolwine, Virginia 24185
TELEPHONE:	(276) 930-1057
E-MAIL:	info@mountainrose-inn.com
WEBSITE:	www.mountainrose-inn.com
ROOMS:	5 Rooms; Private baths
CHILDREN:	Children age 2 and older welcome
ANIMALS:	Not allowed
HANDICAPPED:	Call ahead
DIETARY NEEDS:	Call ahead

Mango Melon Soup

Makes 4 to 6 Servings

"This unique, refreshing soup is a sophisticated way to serve fruit. Presented in a chilled bowl, with a hint of mint, it is sure to please your guests on a hot summer morning." ~ Innkeeper, The Mountain Rose Inn

2   mangoes, peeled, pitted and chopped
2   tablespoons powdered sugar
1   cantaloupe, peeled, seeded and chopped
¼   cup peach Chardonnay (or other sweet white wine)
2   tablespoons chopped fresh mint
2   tablespoons plain yogurt
2   tablespoons fresh lemon juice
Mint sprigs or leaves, for garnish

Purée all ingredients, except mint springs, in a blender; cover and chill for a few hours or overnight. Serve soup in chilled bowls, garnished with fresh mint sprigs or leaves.

Highland Farm & Inn

Once an encampment for Yankee soldiers (isn't that Southern hospitality!) the original summer kitchen for the manor house still remains. The original structure on the Rappahannock River no longer exists, but stones from it were used in the walls and fireplaces of the present house.

After a restful evening in one of the well-appointed suites and a scrumptious country breakfast, take a leisurely stroll through the inn's 36 acres of lovely countryside, walk along the Rappahannock River or ride bikes along quiet country roads. Explore to your heart's content.

INNKEEPERS:	Ralph & Linda Robinson
ADDRESS:	10981 Lee's Mill Road
	Remington, Virginia 22734
TELEPHONE:	(540) 439-0088
E-MAIL:	innkeeper@highlandfarminn.com
WEBSITE:	www.highlandfarminn.com
ROOMS:	2 Rooms; 1 Cottage; Private baths
CHILDREN:	Children age 12 and older welcome
ANIMALS:	Not allowed; Resident dog & horses
HANDICAPPED:	Handicapped accessible
DIETARY NEEDS:	Will accommodate guests' special dietary needs

Creamy Fruit Syrup

Makes 1 Cup

"Everyone asks, 'What is on this fruit – it's so good!' This syrup is light and adds just a bit of sweetness to fresh fruit." - Innkeeper, Highland Farm & Inn

⅓ cup corn syrup
⅓ cup sugar
⅓ cup half & half, cream or whipping cream
1 teaspoon vanilla extract
1 teaspoon almond extract
1 teaspoon grated orange or lemon zest

Combine corn syrup, sugar and half & half in a small saucepan over medium-low heat; heat until sugar is dissolved (do not boil). Remove from heat and cool.

When corn syrup mixture is cool, stir in vanilla and almond extracts and orange or lemon zest. Cover and refrigerate. Drizzle a small amount of creamy fruit syrup over individual servings of fruit, such as berries, peaches, pineapple, melon, etc.

Montclair

The Montclair Bed & Breakfast is a finely restored circa 1880 Italianate townhouse, located in the Stuart Addition of historic downtown Staunton. The inn is listed on the National Register of Historic Places and won the Historic Staunton Foundation's Preservation Award in 1995.

Guests will enjoy the relaxed ambiance of the Fox Hunt décor. Rooms feature antique furnishings and four-poster beds. Period baths feature claw-foot tubs and pedestal sinks. Fireplaces in the parlor, library and dining room create cozy conversation areas.

INNKEEPERS:	Mark & Shari Bang
ADDRESS:	320 North New Street
	Staunton, Virginia 24401
TELEPHONE:	(540) 885-8832; (877) 885-8832
E-MAIL:	mebang@rica.net
WEBSITE:	www.montclairbb.com
ROOMS:	4 Rooms; Private baths
CHILDREN:	Children age 12 and older welcome
ANIMALS:	Not allowed; Resident cat
HANDICAPPED:	Handicapped accessible; 1 room
DIETARY NEEDS:	Will accommodate guests' special dietary needs

Lemon Curd

Makes 2 Cups

"Great for high tea with scones." ~ Innkeeper, Montclair Bed & Breakfast

3   large eggs
1   cup sugar
½   cup fresh lemon juice
Grated zest of 3 large lemons
1   stick unsalted butter, melted

Whisk together eggs, sugar, lemon juice and lemon zest until well combined. Whisk in melted butter. Microwave for 2 minutes, whisking often (the curd should be smooth and coat a wooden spoon). Cool and then store in the refrigerator.

Caldonia Farm ~ 1812

S cenery, history, recreation, accommodations and hospitality all come together beautifully at Caledonia Farm ~ 1812. Farm amenities include a spa, bikes, lawn games, hay rides, bird watching, library, porches and patios. Nearby are antique stores, caves, fishing, wineries, stables, historic battle grounds, canoeing, golf, tennis, swimming and superb dining.

With the renowned Blue Ridge Mountains in the background, Caledonia Farm offers its guests a beautiful setting. Guest rooms feature fine beds, period furnishings and modern comforts.

INNKEEPERS:	Phil Irwin
ADDRESS:	47 Dearing Road
	Flint Hill, Virginia 22627
TELEPHONE:	(540) 675-3693; (800) 262-1812
E-MAIL:	Not available
WEBSITE:	www.bnb1812.com
ROOMS:	2 Suites; Private baths
CHILDREN:	Children age 12 and older welcome
ANIMALS:	Horses welcome
HANDICAPPED:	Not handicapped accessible
DIETARY NEEDS:	Will accommodate guests' special dietary needs

Rhubarb Ginger Sauce

Makes About 3 Cups

3 cups chopped rhubarb
⅓ cup sugar
⅓ cup water
3 tablespoons finely chopped crystallized ginger
⅓ cup orange liqueur

Combine rhubarb, sugar and water in a medium saucepan over medium heat. Bring to a boil, lower heat and simmer, uncovered, stirring often, until mixture is consistency of applesauce. Stir in ginger and liqueur and simmer for 15 minutes (if sauce becomes too thick, thin it with a little bit of water). Cool, then serve on most anything.

Federal Crest Inn

The Federal Crest Inn is just minutes from such historic Civil War sites as Appomattox, the Confederate cemetery and rose gardens, Fort Early, Jefferson's retreat home, the Blue Ridge Mountains, the Point of Honor Museum and the new National D-Day Memorial in Bedford.

Federal red and blue complement the magnificent magnolia blossoms that adorn the Magnolia Suite. The suite features a queen-size, carved four-poster bed, marble antique dresser, fireplace and private Victorian bath.

INNKEEPERS:	Ann & Phil Ripley
ADDRESS:	1101 Federal Street
	Lynchburg, Virginia 24504
TELEPHONE:	(800) 818-6155
E-MAIL:	inn@federalcrest.com
WEBSITE:	www.federalcrest.com
ROOMS:	4 Rooms; 3 Suites; Private baths
CHILDREN:	Children age 10 and older welcome
ANIMALS:	Not allowed; Resident dog
HANDICAPPED:	Not handicapped accessible
DIETARY NEEDS:	Will accommodate guests' special dietary needs

Fancy Fruit Compote

Makes 6 Servings

"A B&B friend served this sauce over fruit at a potluck dinner many years ago. With a few changes, this has become one of our favorites as an opener before our breakfast entrée." ~ Innkeeper, Federal Crest Inn Bed & Breakfast

1	(11-ounce) can mandarin oranges, drained (juice reserved)
1	(20-ounce) can pineapple chunks, drained (juice reserved)
½	cup sugar plus extra for dipping strawberries
2	tablespoons cornstarch
2	tablespoons fresh lemon juice
2	apples, chopped (peeled, if desired)
2	bananas, sliced
1	cup mixed red and green grapes (or sliced kiwi, cherries, etc.)
6	large strawberries, with tops

Combine reserved juice from drained mandarin oranges and pineapple chunks, sugar, cornstarch and lemon juice in a saucepan over medium-low heat. Cook until mixture thickens, then remove from heat and cool.

In a large bowl, combine mandarin oranges, pineapple chunks, apples and bananas. Stir in grapes. Pour cooled sauce over fruit mixture and stir gently to combine. Divide fruit among serving bowls. Place bowls on saucers. Dip whole strawberries in sugar and place 1 strawberry atop each serving. Serve immediately on plates decorated with flowers, if desired.

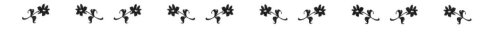

Bluemont

G uest rooms at the Bluemont Bed & Breakfast have all the amenities you might need – plush velour robes, Egyptian and Pima cotton towels, quality linens and thick, billowy comforters. Fresh flowers and chocolates at "turn down" are extra touches to make your room special.

Bluemont Bed & Breakfast is convenient to such attractions as Shenandoah National Park, Luray Caverns and Lake Arrowhead, as well as golf courses, wineries and numerous historic and recreational sites.

INNKEEPERS:	Eleanor & Alfred Ames
ADDRESS:	1852 U.S. Highway Business 340
	Luray, Virginia 22835
TELEPHONE:	(540) 743-1268; (888) 465-8729
E-MAIL:	innkeeper@bluemontbb.com
WEBSITE:	www.bluemontbb.com
ROOMS:	3 Rooms; Private baths
CHILDREN:	Children age 12 and older welcome
ANIMALS:	Not allowed, Resident cats
HANDICAPPED:	Not handicapped accessible
DIETARY NEEDS:	Will accommodate guests' special dietary needs

Morning Peach Wake-up Drink

Makes 4 Servings

"A sparkling, flavorful drink. Guests love it. In fact, one day a fellow called and asked for the recipe for a party he was giving. He couldn't remember the name, but he remembered the peach taste!" ~ Innkeeper, Bluemont Bed & Breakfast

1   (11½-ounce) can Welch's frozen white grape juice
2   grape juice cans water
1   grape juice can crushed ice
1   (8-ounce) container custard-style peach yogurt
½   cup sliced fresh or frozen peaches

Purée all ingredients in a blender. (You may have to purée the drink in 2 batches so as not to overflow the blender – just mix it all in a pitcher after blending.) Serve in fancy glasses, such as wine goblets. The drink can sit for a while before serving, but blend it again to froth it up.

The Black Horse Inn

The Black Horse Inn is a historic hunt-country estate located just 45 minutes from Washington, D.C. This northern Virginia bed & breakfast provides lodging for the most discriminating traveler, with bountiful breakfasts and an afternoon tea.

Recently restored, the inn has eight rooms, all with their own private baths, many with four-poster canopy beds, Jacuzzi tubs and fireplaces. The inn also accommodates horses in their stables for overnight visits.

INNKEEPERS:	Lynn Pirozzoli
ADDRESS:	8393 Meetze Road
	Warrenton, Virginia 20187
TELEPHONE:	(540) 349-4020
E-MAIL:	relax@blackhorseinn.com
WEBSITE:	www.blackhorseinn.com
ROOMS:	8 Rooms; 1 Suite; Private baths
CHILDREN:	Children age 12 and older welcome
ANIMALS:	Horses welcome (overnight stabling); Resident dog
HANDICAPPED:	Not handicapped accessible
DIETARY NEEDS:	Will accommodate guests' special dietary needs

The Perfect Cup of Tea

Makes 5 Cups

"To ensure a great pot of tea, don't brew the tea any longer than the recipe directs or it will be bitter. After brewing, squeeze the tea bags gently – just enough to remove any excess water, but not enough to extract any of the bitter tannins." - Innkeeper, The Black Horse Inn

1	tablespoon whole cloves
3	regular-size black tea bags
4	cups boiling water
½	cup orange juice
⅓	cup honey
¼	cup lime juice

Fill a tea kettle with fresh, cold water and bring it to a rolling boil. Fill a teapot with hot water to warm it (this will encourage the tea leaves to open properly). Empty the hot water out of the teapot.

Put cloves in a tea ball and put tea ball in teapot. Add tea bags to tea pot. Add boiling water, cover and let stand for 5 minutes. Remove tea ball. Remove and discard tea bags, squeezing the tea bags gently just to remove any excess liquid. Stir in orange juice, honey and lime juice. Serve hot.

Desserts

Desserts

Heritage House

The Heritage House Bed & Breakfast is a charming 1837 manor house decorated with antiques and heirlooms. Rooms are warm and inviting after an adventurous day hiking Old Rag Mountain, visiting Luray Caverns or canoeing the Rappahannock river.

In the morning, you will enjoy a sumptuous gourmet breakfast with fresh, local, organic berries or fruit, farm-fresh eggs or waffles with sweet or savory toppings. During the day, enjoy fresh homemade cookies, chat with other guests or read about local history in the parlor.

INNKEEPERS:	Gary & Michelle Schwartz
ADDRESS:	291 Main Street
	Washington, Virginia 22747
TELEPHONE:	(540) 675-3207; (888) 819-8280
E-MAIL:	hhbb@shentel.net
WEBSITE:	www.heritagehousebb.com
ROOMS:	4 Rooms; 1 Suite; Private baths
CHILDREN:	Children age 14 and older welcome
ANIMALS:	Not allowed; Resident dog
HANDICAPPED:	Not handicapped accessible
DIETARY NEEDS:	Will accommodate guests' special dietary needs

Cranberry Lace Cookies

Makes 40 to 50 Cookies

"This recipe has been passed down through our family. The cookies have a wonderful praline taste – you can't eat just one! For a more formal presentation, my mother would roll the warm cookies around the handle of a wooden spoon and dip the tips in chocolate."~ Innkeeper, Heritage House Bed & Breakfast

⅔   cup all-purpose flour
½   teaspoon baking soda
½   teaspoon salt
½   cup old-fashioned rolled oats
1½ sticks unsalted butter, softened
⅔   cup white sugar
⅔   cup packed light brown sugar
1   large egg, lightly beaten
1   teaspoon vanilla extract
2   cups pecan pieces
⅔   cups dried cranberries

Preheat oven to 350°F. In a small bowl, whisk together flour, baking soda and salt. Stir in oats. In a large bowl, cream butter and white and brown sugars until light and fluffy. Beat in egg. Beat in vanilla. Fold in flour mixture. Stir in pecans and cranberries.

Form dough into 1-inch balls and place on a parchment paper-lined or greased baking sheet, about 2½ inches apart. Bake for 7-8 minutes, until golden brown and lacy.

Tree Streets Inn

G uest rooms at the Tree Streets Inn are decorated with specially chosen fabrics and homemade quilts. Adjoining the bedrooms is an enclosed porch, overlooking the pool. In season, take a dip in the secluded pool or just sit on one of the porches in the cool breeze and enjoy the gardens and birds. In fall and winter, relax in front of one of the great fireplaces.

In the morning, you will be treated to a full Southern breakfast in front of the fireplace in the formal dining room.

INNKEEPERS:	William & Nickie Aldridge
ADDRESS:	421 Walnut Avenue
	Waynesboro, Virginia 22980
TELEPHONE:	(540) 949-4484; (877) 378-0456
E-MAIL:	treestreetsinn@ntelos.net
WEBSITE:	www.treestreetsinn.com
ROOMS:	3 Rooms; 1 Suite; Private baths
CHILDREN:	Children age 8 and older welcome
ANIMALS:	Not allowed; Resident dog
HANDICAPPED:	Not handicapped accessible
DIETARY NEEDS:	Will accommodate guests' special dietary needs

Praline Cookies

Makes 10 to 12 Cookies

"My grandmother and mother-in-law always made these cookies. They are thin and crunchy – a nice treat for fall or Mardi Gras time." ~ Innkeeper, Tree Streets Inn Bed & Breakfast

½	cup packed dark brown sugar (or ¼ cup white sugar and ¼ cup packed dark brown sugar)
2	tablespoons all-purpose flour
½	teaspoon salt
2	large egg whites
1	teaspoon vanilla extract
2	cups coarsely chopped pecans

Preheat oven to 275°F. Butter a baking sheet well. Sift together brown sugar, flour and salt into a bowl. In a separate bowl, with a mixer at medium speed, beat egg whites to stiff (but not dry) peaks. Gently fold egg whites and vanilla into brown sugar mixture. Carefully fold in nuts. Drop dough by teaspoonsful onto baking sheet. Bake for 20-25 minutes, until firm. Remove cookies from baking sheet while still warm.

Fountain Hall

The beautiful foothills of the Blue Ridge Mountains are an ideal setting for Fountain Hall, Culpeper's first bed & breakfast. Located in historic downtown Culpeper, the inn boasts ten-foot ceilings, a sweeping walnut staircase, large common rooms and six tastefully appointed guest rooms.

In addition to elegant accommodations and generous hospitality, the inn's prime location in the heart of Virginia's wine country provides guests with marvelous opportunities to explore the area's many treasures.

INNKEEPERS:	Steve & Kathi Walker
ADDRESS:	609 South East Street
	Culpeper, Virginia 22701
TELEPHONE:	(540) 825-8300; (800) 298-4748
E-MAIL:	visit@fountainhall.com
WEBSITE:	www.fountainhall.com
ROOMS:	6 Rooms; Private baths
CHILDREN:	Children age 12 and older welcome
ANIMALS:	Not allowed
HANDICAPPED:	Not handicapped accessible
DIETARY NEEDS:	Will accommodate guests' special dietary needs

Grandma Paterno's Holiday Tea Cookies "Tatalles"

Makes 24 to 30 Cookies

½   cup sugar
5   cups all-purpose flour
3½   teaspoons baking powder
Pinch of salt
7   large eggs
Grated orange zest, to taste
½   teaspoon vanilla extract
½   cup vegetable oil
Candy sprinkles, for garnish

Icing:
1   cup powdered sugar (about)
2   tablespoons fresh lemon juice

Preheat oven to 350°F. In a large bowl, combine flour, sugar, baking powder and salt. Add eggs, orange zest, vanilla and oil; mix well. Roll dough into logs about ¾-inch thick and 4-6 inches long. Pinch ends of logs together, forming crescent shapes. Bake for about 20 minutes, or until light brown. Cool cookies, then dip tops in icing and sprinkle with candy sprinkles.

For the icing: Combine powdered sugar and lemon juice (it should be thick, like molasses).

Nesselrod on the New

N esselrod on the New Gardens & Guesthouse, located on a bluff over-looking the New River, provides lodging in comfortable elegance. The historic, terraced garden, which is nostalgically referred to as the "sunken garden," is the site of many weddings. The sheer drama of white pine columns wrapped with ivy transform the sunken garden into a "cathedral."

In the morning, you will be served a European three-course breakfast, featuring fresh eggs from local farms, imported granola or Scottish oatmeal, a seasonal fruit dish and Virginia specialty items.

INNKEEPERS:	Hal & Cheryl Gillespie
ADDRESS:	7535 Lee Highway
	Radford, Virginia 24141
TELEPHONE:	(540) 731-4970
E-MAIL:	innkeeper@nesselrod.com
WEBSITE:	www.nesselrod.com
ROOMS:	4 Rooms; Private baths
CHILDREN:	Welcome
ANIMALS:	Not allowed
HANDICAPPED:	Not handicapped accessible
DIETARY NEEDS:	Will accommodate guests' special dietary needs

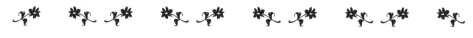

Lemon Ginger Drop Cookies

Makes 36 Cookies

1   stick unsalted butter, softened
¾   cup plus 2 tablespoons sugar plus extra for sprinkling on cookies
1   large egg
1   tablespoon finely grated lemon zest
1⅓   cups all-purpose flour
¼   teaspoon salt
½   teaspoon ground ginger
½   teaspoon baking soda
¼   cup diced crystallized (candied) ginger

Preheat oven to 350°F. Line 2 baking sheets with parchment paper. In a large bowl, mix butter and ¾ cup plus 2 tablespoons of sugar with a mixer at medium-high speed for about 5 minutes. Add egg and mix at high speed. Mix in lemon zest. In a medium bowl, whisk together flour, salt, ground ginger, baking soda and crystallized ginger; add to butter mixture and mix at medium-low speed for about 20 seconds.

Drop 2 teaspoons of batter at a time, about 2 inches apart, onto baking sheets. Bake for 7 minutes. Sprinkle cookies with sugar. Rotate baking sheets and bake for 7 minutes more. Slide parchment paper onto a wire rack and bake cookies for 15 minutes.

The Black Horse Inn

The Black Horse Inn features eight very special and elegant rooms. The Hunter's Haven Room was used as a sleeping porch in the 1850s, and features an exposed rock fireplace, four-poster Chippendale canopy bed, heart-pine floors and hunting lodge décor.

Local activities include horseback riding, fishing and boating, hiking the Appalachian Trail in the Blue Ridge Mountains, wine tasting, hot-air ballooning, golf, aviation shows, watching a fox hunt depart from a nearby manor, steeplechase races, polo, antiquing or just plain relaxing!

INNKEEPERS:	Lynn Pirozzoli
ADDRESS:	8393 Meetze Road
	Warrenton, Virginia 20187
TELEPHONE:	(540) 349-4020
E-MAIL:	relax@blackhorseinn.com
WEBSITE:	www.blackhorseinn.com
ROOMS:	8 Rooms; 1 Suite; Private baths
CHILDREN:	Children age 12 and older welcome
ANIMALS:	Horses welcome (overnight stabling); Resident dog
HANDICAPPED:	Not handicapped accessible
DIETARY NEEDS:	Will accommodate guests' special dietary needs

Lemon Tassies

Makes 24 Tassies

Pearly dollops of whipped cream and a hint of lemon zest dress these tassies for afternoon tea. Serve with the Perfect Cup of Tea (see page 265).

Pastry:
1   stick butter or margarine, softened
1   (3-ounce) package cream cheese, softened
1¼   cups all-purpose flour

Filling:
¾   cup sugar
2   tablespoons cornstarch
½   teaspoon grated lemon zest plus extra, for garnish
½   cup water
⅓   cup fresh lemon juice
1   large egg, lightly beaten
Freshly whipped cream, for serving

For the pastry: Preheat oven to 350°F. Spray mini-muffin cups with non-stick cooking spray. Beat butter and cream cheese with a mixer at medium speed until creamy. Gradually add flour, beating well. Shape pastry into 24 (1-inch) balls; press balls into mini-muffin cups. Bake for 20-22 minutes, or until golden. Cool in pans on wire racks for 10 minutes, then remove from pans and cool completely on wire racks.

For the filling: Combine sugar, cornstarch and lemon zest in a small, heavy saucepan over medium heat. Gradually add water and lemon juice, stirring until blended. Cook over medium heat, stirring constantly, until thickened. Boil for 1 minute, stirring constantly, then remove from heat.

Gradually stir about ¼ of hot sugar mixture into egg; add egg mixture to hot sugar mixture in saucepan, stirring constantly. Cook over medium heat, stirring constantly, for 1 minute, or until thickened. Remove from heat and cool. Cover and chill thoroughly. Spoon chilled filling into pastry shells. Top with whipped cream and a little lemon zest.

The Depot Lodge

E njoy warm hospitality in this historic lodge located in a tranquil village nestled in the scenic Allegheny Mountains. The lodge is housed in a train depot built in 1909. Paint Bank was the final stop of the Potts Valley Branch of the Norfolk and Western Railway.

The Depot Lodge is located on the banks of Potts Creek. Each room offers the soothing sound of flowing water. Rooms are decorated with rustic antique décor and each has its own gas-log stove.

INNKEEPERS:	Mikell Ellison
ADDRESS:	Route 311
	Paint Bank, Virginia 24131
TELEPHONE:	(540) 897-6000; (800) 970-3316
E-MAIL:	mikell@thedepotlodge.com
WEBSITE:	www.thedepotlodge.com
ROOMS:	4 Rooms; 2 Suites; Private baths
CHILDREN:	Welcome
ANIMALS:	Not allowed
HANDICAPPED:	Not handicapped accessible
DIETARY NEEDS:	Will accommodate guests' special dietary needs

Lemon, Nut & White Chocolate Chip Cookies

Makes 36 Cookies

1½ cups all-purpose flour
¾ teaspoon baking soda
½ teaspoon salt
1½ sticks butter or margarine, softened
½ cup packed brown sugar
¼ cup sugar
1 large egg
1 tablespoon lemon juice
1 (12-ounce) package white chocolate chips
1 cup chopped walnuts or cashews
1 teaspoon grated lemon zest

Preheat oven to 350°F. In a medium bowl, combine flour, baking soda and salt. In a large bowl, combine butter and brown and white sugars; beat with a mixer until creamy. Beat in egg and lemon juice. Beat flour mixture into butter mixture a little a time. Stir in white chocolate chips, nuts and lemon zest by hand. Drop dough by rounded tablespoonsful onto a greased baking sheet. Bake for 7-10 minutes. Cool for 3 minutes on the baking sheet, then remove to a wire rack and cool completely.

Harmony Hill

Harmony Hill offers country comforts in a contemporary log home, set on 17 acres of rolling farmland in the foothills of the Blue Ridge Mountains. Guest rooms have private baths, queen-size beds, comfortable furnishings, handmade quilts and ceiling fans. Special touches such as fresh flowers and baskets of fruit in each room make every guest feel pampered.

Breakfast truly is the most important meal of the day. At Harmony Hill, it includes homemade muffins and breads and entrées such as French toast, orange waffles, pumpkin bread pudding or Egg in a Cloud.

INNKEEPERS:	Joanne & Bob Cuoghi
ADDRESS:	929 Wilson Hill Road
	Arrington, Virginia 22922
TELEPHONE:	(434) 263-7750; (877) 263-7750
E-MAIL:	innkeeper@harmony-hill.com
WEBSITE:	www.harmony-hill.com
ROOMS:	5 Rooms; Private baths
CHILDREN:	Children age 6 and older welcome
ANIMALS:	Not allowed
HANDICAPPED:	Not handicapped accessible
DIETARY NEEDS:	Will accommodate guests' special dietary needs

Peanut Butter Chocolate Chip Cookies

Makes 48 Cookies

"These delicious cookies freeze well. For variety, try using half white chocolate chips." ~ Innkeeper, Harmony Hill Bed & Breakfast

2	cups old-fashioned rolled oats
1	cup all-purpose flour
½	teaspoon salt
1	teaspoon baking powder
1	cup chunky peanut butter
1	stick unsalted butter, softened
½	cup packed light brown sugar
½	cup white sugar
3	large eggs, room temperature
1	tablespoon vanilla extract
2	cups semi-sweet or milk chocolate chips
1½	cups shredded coconut

Preheat oven to 350°F. In a medium bowl, combine oats, flour, salt and baking powder. In a large bowl, with a mixer at medium speed, beat peanut butter, butter and brown and white sugars. Add eggs, 1 at a time, beating well after each addition. Beat in vanilla. Gradually beat in oat mixture. Stir in chocolate chips and coconut by hand.

Drop dough by heaping tablespoonsful, spaced about 1-inch apart, onto an ungreased baking sheet. Bake for 15-18 minutes. Remove cookies to a wire rack to cool.

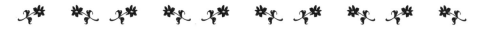

Ridge View

O n the main level of Ridge View, you will enjoy the great room with brick floor, reading area and balcony, the parlor room with television, the dining room and two patios. The Vista del Giardino Room is bright and cheerful, and overlooks the formal garden and garden fountain. The room boasts 1920s vintage furniture and a private bath with whirlpool tub.

For some old-fashioned fun, croquet, horseshoes and boccie are available. Pick fruits, herbs and vegetables from the gardens in season or visit one of the farms in the area.

INNKEEPERS:	Eleanor & Frank Damico
ADDRESS:	Scenic Byway 231
	Rochelle, Virginia 22738
TELEPHONE:	(540) 672-7024
E-MAIL:	edamico@virginia-ridgeview.com
WEBSITE:	www.virginia-ridgeview.com
ROOMS:	3 Rooms; Private baths
CHILDREN:	Welcome
ANIMALS:	Dogs welcome; Call ahead; Resident dogs
HANDICAPPED:	Not handicapped accessible
DIETARY NEEDS:	Will accommodate guests' special dietary needs

Double Chocolate Decadence Biscotti

Makes 48 Biscotti

⅔ cup whole almonds
1 stick butter, softened
¾ cup sugar
2 large eggs
2 tablespoons Amaretto or Kahlúa (or double strength brewed coffee)
2 cups plus 2 tablespoons unbleached all-purpose flour
⅓ cup unsweetened cocoa powder
1½ teaspoons baking power
¼ teaspoon salt
⅔ cup chopped milk chocolate (or mini milk chocolate chips)

Preheat oven to 350°F. Put almonds in a shallow baking pan and bake for 8-10 minutes, until golden brown (watch carefully – they burn easily); set aside to cool. In a large bowl, cream butter and sugar until light and fluffy. Beat in eggs and Amaretto or Kahlúa. In a medium bowl, combine flour, cocoa, baking power and salt; add to butter mixture and mix until blended. Cut almonds into halves or thirds (kitchen shears work well). Fold almonds and milk chocolate into dough.

Lower oven temperature to 325°F. Divide dough in half. On a greased and floured baking sheet, pat each piece of dough into a logs about ½-inch tall, 1½-inches wide and 14-inches long. Space logs at least 2-inches apart. Bake for 30 minutes, or until lightly browned. Transfer to a wire rack and cool for 5 minutes. With a serrated knife, slice logs diagonally on a 45-degree angle about ½-inch thick. Place slices upright on baking sheet, ½-inch apart, and bake for about 15 minutes. Transfer to a wire rack to cool. Store in an air-tight container.

Inn at Tabb's Creek Landing

The Inn at Tabb's Creek Landing was originally the antebellum home of a local sea captain. Built in the 1820s on the banks of Tabb's Creek, the house is surrounded by screened porches and reading rooms.

If you like to fish off the dock, wander manicured paths, luxuriate in the pool, bicycle down country roads, canoe, sunbathe, gaze at a sky filled with countless stars or lose yourself in breathtaking sunsets, then the Inn at Tabb's Creek Landing is for you! The innkeepers are ready with suggestions and can make arrangements for dinner, kayaking, golf or cultural events.

INNKEEPERS:	Bill & Erin Rogers
ADDRESS:	384 Turpin Lane
	Matthews-Port Haywood, Virginia 23138
TELEPHONE:	(804) 725-5136
E-MAIL:	tabbscreeklanding@hotmail.com
WEBSITE:	None available
ROOMS:	4 Rooms; 3 Suites; Private & shared baths
CHILDREN:	Welcome
ANIMALS:	Not allowed
HANDICAPPED:	Handicapped accessible
DIETARY NEEDS:	Will accommodate guests' special dietary needs

Homemade Heath Bars

Makes About 40 Bars

"Make your own Heath Bars at home!" ~ Innkeeper, Inn at Tabb's Creek Landing

1   cup packed brown sugar
2   sticks butter
40   Saltine crackers
1   (12-ounce) package milk chocolate or semi-sweet chocolate chips
Chopped nuts (optional)

Preheat oven to 400°F. Line a jelly-roll pan with foil. Bring brown sugar and butter to a boil in a small saucepan and boil for 3 minutes. Put crackers in a single layer on foil. Pour butter mixture over crackers and bake for 8 minutes. Remove from oven and sprinkle with chocolate chips. Let stand for 5 minutes, then spread chocolate chips over crackers, like a frosting. Sprinkle with nuts, if desired. Let stand until chocolate is set, then break into pieces or slice and serve.

Brierley Hill

The garden at Brierley Hill supplies the inn's dining room with fresh herbs, flowers and vegetables. Spring brings fresh salads of baby lettuces and tiny peas. Neat and tidy most of the year with raised beds and gravel paths, the garden overflows in summer with an abundance of juicy tomatoes, peppers, eggplants, leeks and more.

The Love Seat Suite overlooks the flower and herb garden with its fish pond and fountain. Lacy white linens with cowslip yellow stripes on the king-size, four-poster bed give the room a sunny feeling.

INNKEEPERS:	Ken & Joyce Hawkins
ADDRESS:	985 Borden Road
	Lexington, Virginia 24450
TELEPHONE:	(540) 464-8421; (800) 422-4925
E-MAIL:	relax@brierleyhill.com
WEBSITE:	www.brierleyhill.com
ROOMS:	3 Rooms; 2 Suites; Private baths
CHILDREN:	Children age 12 and older welcome
ANIMALS:	Not allowed; Resident dog
HANDICAPPED:	Not handicapped accessible
DIETARY NEEDS:	Will accommodate guests' special dietary needs

Cherry Nut Bars

Makes 36 Bars

2   cups all-purpose flour
2   cups quick-cooking rolled oats
1½   cups sugar
2½   sticks butter, melted
½   cup chopped pecans
1   teaspoon baking soda
1   (21-ounce) can cherry pie filling
1   cup miniature marshmallows
Vanilla ice cream, for serving

Preheat oven to 350°F. In a large bowl, combine flour, oats, sugar, butter, pecans and baking soda; beat with a mixer at low speed, scraping bowl often, until mixture resembles coarse crumbs. Remove 1½ cups of flour mixture and set aside for topping.

Press remaining flour mixture into an ungreased 9x13-inch baking pan. Bake for 12-15 minutes, or until lightly brown on edges. Gently spoon pie filling evenly over hot, partially baked crust. Sprinkle with marshmallows. Sprinkle with reserved 1½ cups of flour mixture. Bake for 25-35 minutes, or until light brown. Cool and cut into bars.

To make desert squares, cut into 15 bars and top each serving with a scoop of vanilla ice cream.

Nesselrod on the New

N esselrod on the New was designed in the late 1930s by noted architect Everette Fauber, a restoration expert known for his work on the Governor's Palace in Williamsburg and the renovation of the Library of Congress. He was also instrumental in the design of the inn's grounds and the major gardens – the formal boxwood garden and the sunken garden.

No detail is forgotten – from fresh flowers in every room to heated towel racks. Fine robes, Italian linens and goat's milk bath products ensure that you will be pampered.

INNKEEPERS:	Hal & Cheryl Gillespie
ADDRESS:	7535 Lee Highway
	Radford, Virginia 24141
TELEPHONE:	(540) 731-4970
E-MAIL:	innkeeper@nesselrod.com
WEBSITE:	www.nesselrod.com
ROOMS:	4 Rooms; Private baths
CHILDREN:	Welcome
ANIMALS:	Not allowed
HANDICAPPED:	Not handicapped accessible
DIETARY NEEDS:	Will accommodate guests' special dietary needs

English Sticky Toffee Pudding

Makes 6 to 8 Servings

1	cup plus 1 tablespoon all-purpose flour
1	teaspoon baking powder
½	stick plus 3 tablespoons unsalted butter, softened
¾	cup white sugar
1	large egg
¾	cup finely chopped pitted dates
1	teaspoon baking soda
1	teaspoon vanilla extract
1¼	cups boiling water
¼	cup plus 1 tablespoon packed brown sugar
2	tablespoons heavy cream

Whipped cream, for serving

Preheat oven to 350°F. Butter a 9- or 10-inch (1½- to 2-quart) gratin dish or other shallow, oven-proof baking dish. Sift together 1 cup of flour and baking powder onto a sheet of waxed paper. Beat ½ stick of butter and white sugar with a mixer at medium-high speed until light and fluffy. Beat in egg and ¼ of flour mixture. Mix in remaining flour mixture just until combined.

In a small, heat-proof bowl, toss dates with the 1 tablespoon of flour. Add baking soda, vanilla and boiling water; stir well. Stir date mixture into butter mixture and pour into baking dish. Bake pudding on middle rack of oven for 30-40 minutes, until set and golden brown.

Preheat broiler. Combine brown sugar, cream and remaining 3 tablespoons of butter in a small, heavy saucepan over medium-high heat. Bring to a boil, lower heat to low and simmer, stirring constantly, for about 3 minutes, until thickened; pour over hot pudding. Broil pudding about 4 inches from heat for 1 minute, or until top is bubbling. Cool pudding slightly on a wire rack. Serve with whipped cream.

High Meadows Vineyard Inn

The High Meadows Vineyard Inn offers country indulgence at its best, with beautiful gardens, tranquil grounds, incredible Pinot Noir grape vineyards and period restoration. Let the innkeepers pamper you with hot tubs, Jacuzzis and twilight Virginia wine tasting with hors d'oeuvres.

Inn guests can enjoy activities such as exploring Civil War trails, hiking the Blue Ridge Mountains, biking, James River trips, horseback riding, skiing, antique shopping and historic Monticello, Ashlawn and Michie Tavern.

INNKEEPERS:	Rose Farber & Jon Storey
ADDRESS:	55 High Meadows Lane
	Scottsville, Virginia 24590
TELEPHONE:	(434) 286-2218; (800) 232-1832
E-MAIL:	highmeadows@earthlink.net
WEBSITE:	www.highmeadows.com
ROOMS:	12 Rooms; 3 Suites; 3 Cottages; Private baths
CHILDREN:	Welcome
ANIMALS:	Not allowed; Resident dog
HANDICAPPED:	Not handicapped accessible
DIETARY NEEDS:	Will accommodate guests' special dietary needs

Amaretto Cheesecake

Makes 8 to 10 Servings

"Any type of liqueur or liquid can be used to make this light, smooth cheesecake."
~ Innkeeper, High Meadows Vineyard Inn

1	cup graham cracker crumbs
½	stick butter, melted
4	(8-ounce) packages cream cheese, softened
1⅔	cups sugar
5	large eggs
1	teaspoon vanilla extract
1	cup Amaretto or other liqueur

Preheat oven to 350°F. Combine graham cracker crumbs and butter; press into a 9- or 10-inch springform pan. Bake for 10 minutes. Mix cream cheese and sugar until well blended. Add eggs, 1 at a time, mixing well after each addition. Add vanilla and Amaretto; mix well and pour into crust.

Wrap pan tightly with foil (to keep water from seeping into pan) and place in a larger pan filled with about 1 inch of boiling water. Bake cheesecake for 80 minutes. Turn off oven and leave cheesecake in oven for 2 hours. The cheesecake can be unmolded while still warm, but it's easiest if you chill it first.

Victoria & Albert Inn

The Victoria & Albert Inn is located in historic Abingdon, which was established in 1778. The inn is near such attractions as the Barter Theatre, William King Regional Arts Center, Virginia Creeper Trail and Virginia Highlands Festival, as well as specialty shops, fine art galleries, hiking and lakes, rivers and streams for boating, swimming and fishing.

The Blue Room is a sunny, spacious second-floor room furnished with a king-size mahogany rice bed, a writing desk, a Queen Anne chair in the bay window area and a sofa and wing chair.

INNKEEPERS:	Hazel Ramos-Cano & Richard Cano
ADDRESS:	224 Oak Hill Street
	Abingdon, Virginia 24210
TELEPHONE:	(276) 623-1281
E-MAIL:	rcano@naxs.com
WEBSITE:	www.abingdon-virginia.com
ROOMS:	4 Rooms; 1 Suite; Private baths
CHILDREN:	Children age 12 and older welcome
ANIMALS:	Not allowed
HANDICAPPED:	Not handicapped accessible
DIETARY NEEDS:	Will accommodate guests' special dietary needs

Sweet Potato Cheesecake

Makes 8 Servings

"Being a restaurateur as well as an innkeeper, I have the privilege to attend many food shows. I got this recipe from the family of three generations of potato growers in southeastern North Carolina, probably the largest potato producing county in America." ~ Innkeeper, Victoria & Albert Inn

1	cup graham cracker crumbs
½	stick butter, melted
2	tablespoons plus 2 cups sugar
3	(8-ounce) packages cream cheese, softened
1½	pounds sweet potatoes, cooked and mashed
4	large eggs
½	cup all-purpose flour
1-2	teaspoons apple pie spice (or pumpkin pie spice)

Topping:
1	(14-ounce) can sweetened condensed milk
1	cup chopped nuts
1	cup shredded coconut

Preheat oven to 350°F. Spray a 9-inch springform pan with non-stick cooking spray. Combine graham cracker crumbs, butter and 2 tablespoons of sugar; press into pan. Bake for 10 minutes.

Thoroughly mix cream cheese, sweet potatoes, remaining 2 cups of sugar, eggs, flour and apple pie spice; pour into crust. Bake for 45-50 minutes. Cool completely. Spread topping over top of cooled cheesecake. Freeze for 30 minutes, then slice and serve.

For the topping: Combine topping ingredients.

River's Edge

River's Edge is located on the Little River in the Blue Ridge Mountains. With 24 acres at the end of a country road and 1,000 feet of river frontage, the inn offers a beautiful, peaceful and private setting for you to rest and relax.

River's Edge is 30 minutes from Blacksburg, Virginia Tech, Radford and Radford University to the north, and the same distance from the Blue Ridge Parkway to the south.

INNKEEPERS:	Lee Britton
ADDRESS:	6208 Little Camp Road
	Riner, Virginia 24149
TELEPHONE:	(540) 381-4147; (888) 746-9418
E-MAIL:	innkeeper@river-edge.com
WEBSITE:	www.river-edge.com
ROOMS:	4 Rooms; Private baths
CHILDREN:	Welcome
ANIMALS:	Dogs welcome; Resident cats
HANDICAPPED:	Handicapped accessible
DIETARY NEEDS:	Will accommodate guests' special dietary needs

Chocolate Bread Pudding

Makes 6 to 8 Servings

"When I got this recipe from my brother, it called for heavy cream. I have reduced the fat by substituting whole milk for the cream. This has the added benefit of allowing the bread to better absorb the chocolate mixture." ~ Innkeeper, River's Edge

3	large eggs, separated
2	tablespoons plus ½ cup sugar
1½	teaspoons vanilla extract
1½	teaspoons instant coffee granules
1	cup whole milk
2	tablespoons unsalted butter
6	ounces semi-sweet chocolate chips
½	(1-pound) loaf cinnamon bread (such as Pepperidge Farm), cut into 1-inch cubes

Grease a 9x13-inch baking dish. Put egg yolks in a large bowl. Whisk in 2 tablespoons of sugar, vanilla and instant coffee. Bring milk and butter to a simmer in a small, heavy saucepan over medium-high heat, stirring frequently. Slowly whisk a little bit of the milk mixture into the egg yolk mixture, then whisk in the remaining milk mixture.

Melt chocolate in microwave or on stovetop; add to milk mixture and whisk until smooth and combined. In a large bowl, beat egg whites with a mixer at medium speed until soft peaks form. Gradually beat in the ½ cup of sugar until stiff (but not dry) peaks form. Gently fold egg white mixture, ⅓ at a time, into milk mixture. Add bread and toss to coat evenly. Put mixture in baking dish. Cover with foil and let stand for 30 minutes.

Preheat oven to 325°F. Bake bread pudding for about 45 minutes, until set. Serve warm or at room temperature.

Hummingbird Inn

Enjoy country hospitality in a unique Victorian Carpenter Gothic villa in a little Virginia railroad town. The inn is centrally located just west of scenic Goshen Pass on the western edge of the Shenandoah Valley, in a small triangle defined by Lexington, Warm Springs/Hot Springs and Staunton.

Outside the inn, over an acre of landscaped grounds, with over a thousand perennials and shrubs, makes for pleasant strolling. Within five minutes of the inn, you'll find Goshen Pass, a spectacular rocky gorge with one of the finest vistas in Virginia. Dozens of miles of hiking trails can be found there.

INNKEEPERS:	Pam Miller & Dick Matthews
ADDRESS:	30 Wood Lane
	Goshen, Virginia 24439
TELEPHONE:	(540) 997-9065; (800) 397-3214
E-MAIL:	stay@hummingbirdinn.com
WEBSITE:	www.hummingbirdinn.com
ROOMS:	5 Rooms; Private baths
CHILDREN:	Children age 12 and older welcome
ANIMALS:	Well-behaved dogs welcome
HANDICAPPED:	Not handicapped accessible
DIETARY NEEDS:	Will accommodate guests' special dietary needs

Beulah's Banana Pecan Cake

Makes 4 Servings

"Our neighbor, Beulah Kirby, brought us this cake when we first bought the inn. We asked for the recipe and have been serving it to our guests ever since."
~ Innkeeper, Hummingbird Inn

1½	cups canola oil
1½	cups sugar
3	large eggs
3	cups all-purpose flour
1	teaspoon salt
1	teaspoon baking soda
1	tablespoon vanilla extract
½	cup evaporated milk
1½	cups mashed banana (about 3 bananas)
1	cup chopped pecans

Preheat oven to 350°F. Grease and floured a Bundt pan. In a large bowl, combine oil and sugar. Add eggs and mix well. Sift together flour, salt and baking soda into a medium bowl; add to oil mixture and mix well. Add vanilla and evaporated milk; mix well. Mix in bananas. Mix in pecans.

Pour batter into pan. Bake for 60 minutes, or until a toothpick inserted in center comes out clean. Serve warm or at room temperature.

Note: The finished cake freezes well.

The Inn at Warner Hall

Established in 1642, the Inn at Warner Hall reflects more than 350 years of history and architectural development. Today, Warner Hall welcomes guests in the lasting tradition of fine Southern hospitality. Completely renovated and lovingly restored, the inn offers guests a rare opportunity to experience the best of the Old World with modern amenities.

Enter through a hall with a grand central staircase, dividing as it rises to the guest rooms above. French doors lead from the casually elegant drawing and dining rooms to the dramatic glass- amy screen-enclosed river porch.

INNKEEPERS:	Theresa & Troy Stavens
ADDRESS:	4750 Warner Hall Road
	Gloucester, Virginia 23061
TELEPHONE:	(804) 695-9565; (800) 331-2720
E-MAIL:	whall@inna.net
WEBSITE:	www.warnerhall.com
ROOMS:	9 Rooms; 2 Suites; Private baths
CHILDREN:	Children age 8 and older welcome
ANIMALS:	Not allowed; Resident dog
HANDICAPPED:	Handicapped accessible
DIETARY NEEDS:	Will accommodate guests' special dietary needs

Orange Pound Cake

Makes 1 (9-inch) Cake

"This cake is good to serve with fruit sauces or whipped cream." ~ Chef Eric
Garcia, The Inn at Warner Hall

1½ sticks butter, softened
1   cup sugar
Grated zest of 2 oranges
1   teaspoon vanilla extract
3   large eggs, room temperature
1½ cups all-purpose flour
1   teaspoon baking powder
Pinch of salt

Glaze:
Juice of 2 oranges
⅓   cup sugar

Preheat oven to 350°F. Butter and flour a 9-inch springform pan. In a large
bowl, cream butter, sugar and orange zest with a mixer at medium-high
speed. Beat in vanilla at medium-low speed. Add eggs, 1 at a time, mixing
well after each addition. Sift together flour, baking powder and salt into a
medium bowl. Beat flour mixture into butter mixture, a little at a time (do
not overmix). Pour batter into pan.

Bake cake for about 60 minutes, or until a toothpick inserted in center
comes out clean. Cool cake in pan for 10-15 minutes, then remove sides of
pan and place cake on a large plate. With a toothpick, poke about 30 holes
in cake. Spoon glaze over cake. Cool cake to room temperature, then slice
and serve.

For the glaze: While cake is cooling, combine orange juice and sugar (do
not dissolve sugar by overmixing).

The Inn at Sugar Hollow Farm

The Inn at Sugar Hollow Farm is a country retreat, set on 70 acres and surrounded by picturesque mountains, majestic hardwood forests and rushing woodland streams. The inn is located west of Charlottesville, adjacent to the Blue Ridge Mountains and Shenandoah National Park, and a short drive from Monticello and the University of Virginia.

"I am refreshed, fulfilled and eager to come back. The gentle peacefulness, quiet for thinking and reading, and excursions in the mountains and on trails leaves nothing to be desired." ~ Guest, Inn at Sugar Hollow Farm

INNKEEPERS:	Dick & Hayden Cabell
ADDRESS:	PO Box 5705
	Charlottesville, Virginia 22905
TELEPHONE:	(434) 823-7086
E-MAIL:	innkeeper@sugarhollow.com
WEBSITE:	www.sugarhollow.com
ROOMS:	7 Rooms; Private baths
CHILDREN:	Children age 12 and older welcome
ANIMALS:	Not allowed
HANDICAPPED:	Not handicapped accessible
DIETARY NEEDS:	Will accommodate guests' special dietary needs

Laura's Fresh Apple Cake with Warm Bourbon Sauce

Makes 16 Servings

1½	cups vegetable oil
2	cups sugar
1	teaspoon vanilla extract
3	eggs
3	cups flour (2 cups whole-wheat plus 1 cup all-purpose flour or any combination to equal 3 cups of flour)
1	teaspoon salt
1	teaspoon cinnamon
1	teaspoon baking soda
1	teaspoon nutmeg
3	cups diced or shredded peeled apples
1	cup chopped walnuts
1	cup raisins

Bourbon sauce:

½	stick butter
1	cup packed brown sugar
1	cup half & half or heavy cream, warmed
¼	cup bourbon or brandy

Preheat oven to 350°F. Grease and flour a Bundt pan. In a large bowl, beat together oil, sugar and vanilla. Add eggs and beat until light. Sift together flour, salt, cinnamon, baking soda and nutmeg into a medium bowl. Stir flour mixture into oil mixture. Stir in apples, walnuts and raisins; pour into pan. Bake for 75 minutes, or until a toothpick inserted in center comes out clean. Cool cake slightly, then remove from pan. Serve cake warm, drizzled with warm bourbon sauce.

For the bourbon sauce: Combine butter, brown sugar and half & half in a saucepan over low heat; cook, stirring, until butter in melted and combined. Add bourbon or brandy and beat with a whisk until smooth.

Holladay House

The Holladay House Bed & Breakfast features six guest rooms furnished with family heirlooms and Victorian and Colonial antiques, including four-poster beds, antique marble-top dressers and rocking chairs. The Ivy Suite features a luxurious bath area with a two-person whirlpool tub and a two-person walk-in shower. A private brick patio adjoins the room.

The large, formal dining room sets the mood for a sumptuous, candlelit, three-course breakfast. Antique Havilland china, Fostoria crystal, sterling silver and classical music complete a dining experience to be savored.

INNKEEPERS:	Judy Geary
ADDRESS:	155 West Main Street
	Orange, Virginia 22960
TELEPHONE:	(540) 672-4893; (800) 358-4422
E-MAIL:	jgearyhh@aol.com
WEBSITE:	www.holladayhousebandb.com
ROOMS:	4 Rooms; 2 Suites; Private baths
CHILDREN:	Children age 12 and older welcome
ANIMALS:	Welcome; Resident cats
HANDICAPPED:	Not handicapped accessible
DIETARY NEEDS:	Will accommodate guests' special dietary needs

Colonial Virginia Carrot Cake

Makes 1 (10-inch) Tube Cake

*"This carrot cake tops all the rest – super moist and delicious." - Innkeeper,
Holladay House Bed & Breakfast*

1¼	cups vegetable oil
2	cups sugar
2	cups sifted all-purpose flour
2	teaspoons baking powder
1	teaspoon baking soda
2	teaspoons cinnamon
1	teaspoon salt
4	large eggs
3	generous cups grated carrot
1	cup finely chopped pecans

Cream cheese frosting:

1	(8-ounce) package cream cheese, softened
½	stick butter or margarine, softened
1	pound powdered sugar
1	teaspoon maple or almond extract
1	teaspoon vanilla extract

Preheat oven to 325°F. Grease a 10-inch tube cake pan. In a large bowl, combine oil and sugar. In a medium bowl, combine flour, baking powder, baking soda, cinnamon and salt. Add ½ of flour mixture to oil mixture; mix well. Add remaining flour mixture alternately with eggs (1 egg at a time), mixing well after each addition. Add carrots and mix well. Stir in pecans. Pour batter into pan. Bake for 70 minutes, or until a toothpick inserted in center comes out clean. Cool cake in pan. Frost with cream cheese frosting, if desired.

For the frosting: Combine all frosting ingredients and mix until smooth and well blended.

Long Hill

Long Hill Bed & Breakfast combines the comforts of a modern house with the heritage of the area's building materials. The doors, including their antique hardware, are from demolished houses; the kitchen cabinets were made from pine floor boards from a country store; and the beautiful stained-glass windows framing the foyer came from a church and a house in Richmond.

"I've travelled all over the world many times. By far, Long Hill B&B is five-star." ~ Guest, Long Hill Bed & Breakfast

INNKEEPERS:	George & Rhoda Kriz
ADDRESS:	547 Apple Pie Ridge Road
	Winchester, Virginia 22603
TELEPHONE:	(540) 450-0341; (866) 450-0341
E-MAIL:	longhillbb@longhillbb.com
WEBSITE:	www.longhillbb.com
ROOMS:	3 Rooms; Private baths
CHILDREN:	Not allowed
ANIMALS:	Not allowed
HANDICAPPED:	Handicapped accessible
DIETARY NEEDS:	Will accommodate guests' special dietary needs

Pineapple Bubble Cake

Makes 1 (9x13-inch) Cake

"This has been a family favorite for years – easy to prepare and delicious." ~
Innkeeper, Long Hill Bed & Breakfast

1½   cups all-purpose flour
2   large eggs
1½   cups plus ⅔ cup of sugar
1   cup drained crushed pineapple
1½   teaspoons baking soda
½   cup pineapple juice
½   cup evaporated milk
½   teaspoon vanilla extract
1   stick margarine
½   teaspoon almond extract

Preheat oven to 325°F. Thoroughly combine flour, eggs, 1½ cups of sugar, crushed pineapple, baking soda and pineapple juice; pour into an ungreased 9x13-inch baking pan. Bake for 30 minutes, or until a toothpick inserted in center comes out clean.

When cake is nearly done, combine evaporated milk, vanilla, margarine, almond extract and the ⅔ cup of sugar in a small saucepan over medium heat. Bring to a boil, then pour and spread over hot cake.

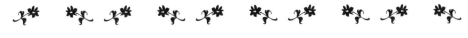

Thornrose House at Gypsy Hill

Thornrose House at Gypsy Hill offers five distinctively decorated guest rooms named for English localities, a guest parlor with overstuffed sofa and chairs, Oriental rugs and family heirlooms, a wrap-around veranda and spacious grounds and gardens for strolling or just relaxing.

A heart-healthy breakfast fit for a king is served in the main dining room on Staffordshire plates, with each plate depicting a different British castle. The house specialty is Otis' Bricher-Muesli with seasonal fruits. Entrées include banana pecan pancakes, egg soufflés, waffles and French toast.

INNKEEPERS:	Otis & Suzy Huston
ADDRESS:	531 Thornrose Avenue
	Staunton, Virginia 24401
TELEPHONE:	(540) 885-7026; (800) 861-4338
E-MAIL:	innkeeper@thornrosehouse.com
WEBSITE:	www.thornrosehouse.com
ROOMS:	5 Rooms; Private baths
CHILDREN:	Children age 5 and older welcome
ANIMALS:	Not allowed; Resident cats
HANDICAPPED:	Not handicapped accessible
DIETARY NEEDS:	Will accommodate guests' special dietary needs

Zucchini Chocolate Spice Cake

Makes 4 Mini Loaves

"We always plant a small vegetable garden, and each year we find ourselves desperately looking for creative ways to use all the zucchini that grows! This cake is great served for afternoon tea." ~ Innkeeper, Thornrose Inn at Gypsy Hill

½	cup canola oil
1	stick butter, softened
1¾	cups packed brown sugar
1	teaspoon vanilla extract
2	large eggs
1½	cups unbleached all-purpose flour
¼	cup unsweetened cocoa powder
½	teaspoon baking powder
1	teaspoon baking soda
½	teaspoon cinnamon
½	teaspoon salt

Pinch of ground cloves
½   cup buttermilk or plain yogurt
2   cups shredded unpeeled zucchini
Powdered sugar, for garnish

Preheat oven to 350°F. Grease 4 mini-loaf pans. In a large bowl, cream oil, butter, brown sugar and vanilla. Add eggs and beat well. In a medium bowl, combine flour, cocoa, baking powder, baking soda, cinnamon, salt and cloves. Add flour mixture alternately with buttermilk or yogurt to butter mixture, stirring well after each addition. Fold in zucchini. Pour batter into pans. Bake for 30-35 minutes, or until a toothpick inserted in center comes out clean. Dust with powdered sugar, if desired.

Newport House

E ach spacious bedroom at the Newport House Bed & Breakfast has a four-poster canopy bed with historically authentic blankets. A full breakfast includes delicious dishes made from authentic Colonial recipes with fruit and honey from the innkeepers' garden, and an interesting historical seminar by your hosts.

Innkeeper John Fitzhugh Millar is a former museum director and captain of a historic, full-rigged ship. He built full-size, operational copies of two Revolutionary War ships for the American bicentennial celebration.

INNKEEPERS:	John & Cathy Millar
ADDRESS:	710 South Henry Street
	Williamsburg, Virginia 23185
TELEPHONE:	(757) 229-1775; (877) 565-1775
E-MAIL:	info@newporthousebb.com
WEBSITE:	www.newporthousebb.com
ROOMS:	2 Rooms; Private baths
CHILDREN:	Welcome
ANIMALS:	Not allowed; Resident rabbit
HANDICAPPED:	Not handicapped accessible
DIETARY NEEDS:	Will accommodate guests' special dietary needs

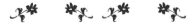

Colonial Chocolate Cake "Pécoul" 1769

Makes 1 (9-inch) Cake

"Chocolate in the Colonial period was almost always a drink, but this cake recipe is said to have celebrated the construction of Pécoul Plantation in Martinique in 1769. The plantation was inherited and beautifully restored by my brother-in-law, the Vicomte D'Origny." ~ Innkeeper, Newport House Bed & Breakfast

9   ounces (about 1¾ cups) chocolate chips
3   tablespoons water
1¼ sticks butter, melted
4   large eggs, separated
1½ cups sugar
3   tablespoons all-purpose flour

Preheat oven to 400°F. Grease and flour a 9-inch round cake pan. Melt chocolate and water in a large saucepan over low heat, stirring until smooth. Stirring constantly, mix in butter and egg yolks. Mix in sugar, then remove from heat.

Beat egg whites with a mixer at medium speed until stiff; fold into chocolate mixture. Stir in flour. Pour batter into pan. Bake for 10 minutes. Lower heat to 325°F and bake for 20 minutes more.

Note: This cake is so gooey that it is often easier to serve it from the pan.

Hummingbird Inn

The Hummingbird Inn was built in 1780. The inn has long been noted for its hospitality, hosting such celebrities as Eleanor Roosevelt and Efraim Zimbalist, Sr. Architectural features include wrap-around verandas on the first and second stories, original pine floors, a rustic den with stone fireplace and a solarium. A deck, next to the old barn which was once the town livery stable, overlooks a wide trout stream.

Whether you're looking for peace and quiet, convivial surroundings or a haven that feels like home, you will find it here.

INNKEEPERS:	Pam Miller & Dick Matthews
ADDRESS:	30 Wood Lane
	Goshen, Virginia 24439
TELEPHONE:	(540) 997-9065; (800) 397-3214
E-MAIL:	stay@hummingbirdinn.com
WEBSITE:	www.hummingbirdinn.com
ROOMS:	5 Rooms; Private baths
CHILDREN:	Children age 12 and older welcome
ANIMALS:	Well-behaved dogs welcome
HANDICAPPED:	Not handicapped accessible
DIETARY NEEDS:	Will accommodate guests' special dietary needs

Chocolate Pothole Cake

Makes 1 Cake

"This recipe came from my mom, who called it 'crazy cake' because you dump all of the ingredients together. I added the cream cheese filling to remind me of the 'pot hole' cupcakes we used to get. Wrapping the cake around the filling makes it all very moist and decadent." - Innkeeper, Hummingbird Inn

Filling:

1	(8-ounce) package cream cheese, softened
1	egg
⅓	cup sugar
⅛	teaspoon salt
6	ounces chocolate chips

Cake:

1	cup unsweetened cocoa powder
2	cups sugar
3	cups all-purpose flour
2	teaspoons baking powder
2	teaspoons baking soda
1	cup canola oil
1	cup sour milk or buttermilk* (to make sour milk, see page 37)
1	cup hot water
3	large eggs
½	teaspoon salt
1	teaspoon vanilla extract

For the filling: Combine all filling ingredients and set aside.

For the cake: Preheat oven to 350°F. Grease and flour a Bundt pan. Mix all cake ingredients well. Pour just over ½ of batter into pan. Top with filling, then top with remaining batter. Bake for about 60 minutes, or until a toothpick inserted in center comes out clean. Cool cake in pan for a few minutes, then remove cake from pan and cool completely.

Note: If you want a rich, dense chocolate cake without the filling, omit the filling and bake it for 45-50 minutes. Remove from pan immediately.

Bed & Breakfast at Foxgloves

B ed & Breakfast at Foxgloves has a stately library with a fireplace and ample reading materials. You may wish to bring your bicycles, cross-country skis, snowshoes and hiking boots. In addition, tennis, horseshoe and shuffleboard courts are provided for your enjoyment.

Other nearby activities include trail riding, wineries, antique shopping, historic sites, Shenandoah National Park, Great Meadow polo matches, Gold Cup Championships, point-to-point racing and superb dining.

INNKEEPERS:	Marcia & Terry Moffat
ADDRESS:	11221 Crest Hill Road
	Marshall, Virginia 20115
TELEPHONE:	(540) 364-4499
E-MAIL:	foxgloves@erols.com
WEBSITE:	www.foxgloves.net
ROOMS:	3 Rooms; Private baths
CHILDREN:	Children age 12 and older welcome
ANIMALS:	Not allowed; Resident dogs & cats
HANDICAPPED:	Not handicapped accessible
DIETARY NEEDS:	Will accommodate guests' special dietary needs

Texas Oil Cake

Makes 1 (9x13-inch) Cake

"This is a rich chocolate cake that has no eggs. Serve with sweetened whipped cream." ~ Innkeeper, Bed & Breakfast at Foxgloves

3	cups all-purpose flour
2	cups sugar
2	teaspoon baking soda
1	teaspoon salt
¼	cup plus 2 tablespoons unsweetened cocoa powder
¾	cup corn oil
2	teaspoons vanilla extract
2	teaspoons white vinegar
2	cups cold water

Sweetened whipped cream, for serving

Preheat oven to 350°F. Mix all ingredients, except water, with a fork in an ungreased 9x13-inch baking pan. Make 3 depressions ("oil wells") in batter. Add water and mix well. Bake for 35 minutes. Serve with whipped cream.

Geographical Listing of Bed & Breakfasts

Alphabetical Listing of Bed & Breakfasts

Recipe Index

About the Author

Melissa Craven was the oldest child in a career Air Force family. She lived in the Tidewater, Virginia area for four years, which was the longest time she ever called a base home. Because of her childhood travels, Melissa was introduced to a variety of culinary styles. As an adult, she is not afraid to try new things in the kitchen. With a background in journalism, recipe testing, marketing and public relations she understands the need for clear and concise recipes. As a cook, she understands the joy that comes from creating a memorable meal for family and friends. Her melding of the two help create a winning recipe. Melissa is also the author of the Colorado Farmers' Market Cookbook and a contributing editor to each of the other books in the Bed & Breakfast Cookbook Series. Melissa now lives with her husband, Chad, and their black and chocolate labs in Denver, Colorado.

The Bed & Breakfast Cookbook Series

Entertain with ease and flair! B&B's and Country Inns from across the nation share their best and most requested recipes.

California Bed & Breakfast Cookbook
127 California B&B's and Country Inns. Book #5 in the series.
$19.95 / 328pp / ISBN 1-889593-11-7

Colorado Bed & Breakfast Cookbook
88 Colorado B&B's and Country Inns. Book #1 in the series. New 2nd ed!
$19.95 / 320pp / ISBN 0-9653751-0-2

New England Bed & Breakfast Cookbook
107 B&B's and Country Inns in CT, MA, ME, NH, RI & VT. Book #6.
$19.95 / 320pp / ISBN 1-889593-12-5

North Carolina Bed & Breakfast Cookbook
70 North Carolina B&B's and Country Inns. Book #7 in the series. New!
$19.95 / 320pp / ISBN 1-889593-08-7

Texas Bed & Breakfast Cookbook
70 Texas B&B's, Guest Ranches and Country Inns. Book #3 in the series.
$19.95 / 320pp / ISBN 1-889593-07-9

Virginia Bed & Breakfast Cookbook
95 Virginia B&B's and Country Inns. Book #4 in the series. New 2nd ed.
$19.95 / 320pp / ISBN 1-889593-04-1

Washington State Bed & Breakfast Cookbook
72 Washington B&B's and Country Inns. Book #2 in the series. New 2nd ed!
$19.95 / 320pp / ISBN 1-889593-05-2

Coming Soon: *Georgia, New York & Pennsylvania* (Spring, 2006).

Bed & Breakfast Cookbook Series
Order Form

2969 Baseline Road, Boulder CO 80303
888.456.3607 • www.3dpress.net • orders@3dpress.net

PLEASE SEND ME:	Price	Quantity
CALIFORNIA BED & BREAKFAST COOKBOOK	$19.95	_____
COLORADO BED & BREAKFAST COOKBOOK	$19.95	_____
NEW ENGLAND BED & BREAKFAST COOKBOOK	$19.95	_____
NORTH CAROLINA BED & BREAKFAST COOKBOOK	$19.95	_____
TEXAS BED & BREAKFAST COOKBOOK	$19.95	_____
VIRGINIA BED & BREAKFAST COOKBOOK	$19.95	_____
WASHINGTON STATE BED & BREAKFAST COOKBOOK	$19.95	_____

SUBTOTAL: $ _____

Colorado residents add 3.8% sales tax. Denver residents add 7.2% $ _____

Add $5.00 for shipping for 1st book, add $1 for each additional $ _____

TOTAL ENCLOSED: $ _____

***Special offer: Buy any 2 books in the series and take a 10% discount.
Buy any 4 or more books and take a 25% discount!**

SEND TO:

Name _____

Address_____

City _____State _____Zip _____

Phone_____A gift from: _____

We accept checks, money orders, Visa or Mastercard. Please make checks payable to 3D Press, Inc.

Please charge my   ☐ VISA   ☐ MASTERCARD

Card Number _____Expiration Date_____